To Ralph

Peace

Richie Jean Sherrod Jackson

The House by the Side of the Road

Home of Dr. and Mrs. Sullivan Jackson, 1416 Lapsley Street, Selma, Alabama, the "house by the side of the road." Courtesy of the author.

The House by the Side of the Road

The Selma Civil Rights Movement

Richie Jean Sherrod Jackson

THE UNIVERSITY OF ALABAMA PRESS
Tuscaloosa

The recipe in this book is intended to be followed
as written by the author. Results will vary.

Library of Congress Cataloging-in-Publication Data
Jackson, Richie Jean Sherrod, 1932–
The house by the side of the road : the Selma civil rights movement / Richie Jean
Sherrod Jackson.
p. cm.
Includes index.
ISBN 978-0-8173-1694-5 (cloth : alk. paper) — ISBN 978-0-8173-8326-8
(electronic) 1. Jackson, Richie Jean Sherrod, 1932– 2. Jackson, Richie Jean
Sherrod, 1932—Homes and haunts—Alabama—Selma. 3. African American
women civil rights workers—Alabama—Selma—Biography. 4. Civil rights
workers—Alabama—Selma—Biography. 5. African Americans—Alabama—
Selma—Biography. 6. African Americans—Civil rights—Alabama—Selma—
History—20th century. 7. Civil rights movements—Alabama—Selma—
History—20th century. 8. Selma (Ala.)—Biography. 9. Selma (Ala.)—Race
relations—History—20th century. I. Title.
F334.S4J28   2011
323.092—dc22
[B]

2010031632

Dedication

This book is dedicated to the memory of my late husband,
Dr. Sullivan Jackson, with whom I shared forty-six wonderful
years in the house by the side of the road, and to our wonderful
daughter Jawana who supported and encouraged me to write
and finish this work.

Contents

Acknowledgments

I would like to thank God for my memory and for as many friends and companions as I can reach through this book, for what they did to make the Selma civil rights movement a success—those who came from all over the country, those who walked to Selma, those who drove, those who flew or came by bus, and those who sent money and supplies. Most of all I would like to thank those that sent up prayers.

I would also like to thank my friend and photographer Randy Williams, who helped me and contributed photographs for the book.

Introduction

In the South the month of March is a beautiful time of year, as winter lets go its grip and Spring is slowly pushing her way in. It's March now as I write this, back in my home in Selma after recovering from illness in the good care of my daughter Jawana at her home in Atlanta. Looking out into my backyard from where I like to sit when I'm home alone, I remember a spring day just like this one, almost fifty years gone. I was enjoying the sight of the new green leaves on the trees in our yard as they replaced the darker green of last year's leaves. I was home alone then also, my husband was at his office, my little daughter was off visiting her grandmother, and I was beginning to settle into the quiet so different from the energy and noise that had ruled in our house for months.

Interrupting the quiet, I heard a car door shut behind the house, soon followed by the doorbell. I wasn't expecting anyone but as I got to the door I saw the familiar old blue Pontiac. It was Martin. I looked past him for the cluster of young committed staff members who were always at his side, day and night, but none of them were there. For a moment I thought he might have come with Ralph Abernathy or Andy Young for some high-level planning, but no, he was alone.

I had never seen Martin like this. He would often sit deep in thought while his staff and local leaders came and went and argued out a problem in front of him, waiting for his decision, but he wasn't going over something in his mind. He looked worn down, exhausted, almost asleep on his feet. "Where is everyone?" I asked.

He then looked at me without his usual warm smile and replied, "I just had to get away. I am so tired, and your house is the only place I could think of where I can be left alone, get some sleep, and be by myself to think."

I opened the door and told him, "Martin, you know this home is always open to you. You're family. Come on in. You know where everything is, take the room you want. We'll see that no one bothers you."

The House by the Side of the Road

I

The Blueprint of My Life
and the House

There is a single thread going through my life, from the very beginning that leads to the house by the side of the road. I believe that when we are born God has a certain plan for our lives—a sort of blueprint. Sometimes the plan may not be seen in our lifetime. We may be the lifeline to a greater person, or a person that will provide a piece in the greater mosaic of God's intentions.

God gave each of us the gift of thought, and as individuals we are each free to alter the plan with the decisions we make as we travel life's path.

Let me stop here and share with you a poem that has been a tremendous influence in my life.

There are hermit souls that live withdrawn
In the place of their self content;
There are souls like stars, that dwell apart,
In a fellowless firmament;
There are pioneer souls that blaze their paths,
Where highways never ran;

But let me live by the side of the road
And be a friend to man.

Let me live in a house by the side of the road
Where the race of men go by
The men who are good and the men who are bad,
As good and as bad as I.
I should not sit in the scorner's seat,
Or hurl the cynic's ban;
Let me live in a house by the side of the road
And be a friend to man.

I see from my house by the side of the road
Where the race of men go by
The men who press with ardor of hope,
The men who are faint with the strife.
But I turn not away from their smiles nor their tears,
Both parts of an infinite plan;
Let me live in a house by the side of the road
And be a friend of man.

I know there are brook-gladdened meadows ahead
And mountains of wearisome heights;
That the road passes on through the long afternoon
And stretches away into the night.
But still I rejoice when the travelers rejoice,
And weep with the strangers that moan,
Nor live in my house by the side of the road
Like a man who dwells alone.

Let me live in my house by the side of the road
It's here the race of men go by,
They are good, they are bad, they are weak, they are strong,
Wise, foolish—so am I;
Then why should I sit in the scorner's seat
Or hurl the cynic's ban?
Let me live in my house by the side of the road
And be a friend to man.

—Sam Walter Foss, 1899

Let me tell you about the house by the side of the road where I live. Even better let me be the voice that tells the story that these walls would tell if they could speak.

I was born in Mobile, Alabama, on August 30, 1932, to Juanita Barnett Richardson and John William Sherrod. Both parents were natives of Sumter County in the west Alabama Black Belt. Both came from small but nurturing Alabama communities. My mother is from Hamner and my father from York, small towns where everyone knows one another.

My father was a brakeman on the Alabama-Tennessee and Northern Railroad, a plum of a job for a black man in the 1930s. I can remember as a small child my mother taking me to the last stop before the train reached York so I could ride the train into the station with my daddy. What a wonderful life this was—pure and simple. I also wanted to look like my daddy, so the smallest pair of overalls was purchased although my mother still had to do a lot of alterations to make them fit. To complete the outfit, I had my very own brakeman's hat and lunch pail filled with a lunch my mother had prepared for the day! I was so excited before the planned trip. I was "off" to work with my daddy. I sat in the caboose with the other members of the crew, each of whom welcomed me with open arms. A father somehow has a special place for his little girl, and I was indeed special to mine.

My mother, who lived to be 102 years old, had seen it all. How many times over the years did I hear her say, "I never thought I would live to see this or that happen." Having to sit in the back on trains and buses and go to separate toilets, not being able to try on clothes because of your color, to have to drink out of a "colored" water fountain. All of this was part of her life. She often stated, "Everyone just knew their place."

My parents, just as their parents had, tried to make life and its experiences better. They knew the bumps we would find along the road, the hatred and division that existed. They tried to protect me from that as much as they could. I was taught that I was no better than anyone else, and there was no one better than I was. They wanted the best for me, and for me to be my best—to be better than those who are filled with hate, to get an education, to be ready for opportunity. Yes, I did run into people who called me "nigger," and I knew what it felt like to have to enter a theater after the whites were seated and then to sit separately upstairs. I knew something about this was wrong, but there was only one theater in town. Yes, I knew segregation well. In York the black schools had a split session so the children could help pick cotton in the fields; the white schools stayed open. My parents had to send me away to school to get a full year's education, first to Selma and then to Washington, D.C.

I also felt Jim Crow when he got personal: once traveling to Washington on the train, I sat near a couple who owned one of the best dress shops in Selma; when my mother or I went in their store, they were all smiles and full of "glad to see you" and "let me help you."

On the train they looked right into my eyes and would not smile or speak.

Nevertheless my family did fare better than some. My father was able to buy my mother a full-length mink coat in the 1930s, and he sought to give my mother and me the best that life could offer at that time. After my mother was given the coat, she was advised that she could not wear that coat in York, Alabama! So she wore it when she and my father would go to Mobile, Selma, and other bigger towns. She seemed to be able to get away with wearing the coat in these places.

My mother's family in the late 1800s did have a very different experience than most blacks in the South at that time. Her father, my grandfather Tom Richardson, was the first Negro postmaster in the state of Alabama and was a registered voter in Sumter County even in the early 1900s. He was also the owner of several hundred acres of land so they were considered "good livers" and were afforded a few extra privileges. He believed that education was the route to better opportunities, that we should become professionals as educators and doctors, even if we were still just "niggers" to some, including some that were related to us.

After I was born, I spent the first four years of my life in Mobile. My father's base was then changed to York. Because my father was originally from York and as his parents were getting up in age, my parents decided to move to York. We lived with them in a house high on a hill. That hill was in many ways the hub of the community. Much of the land on that hill was owned by my paternal grandfather, Jim Sherrod. He and his parents had lived there for more years than I know.

Jim Sherrod's father, my great-grandfather, had given the land that would house the First Baptist Church in York. I remember that

church so well, a block-style building built high, with twelve to fifteen steps leading to the sanctuary, with the Sunday school rooms
on the ground level. The sound of rain hitting the long gable roof of
bright tin, and the preacher and good sisters and brothers singing,
shouting, and saying amen, are sounds etched into my memory. Services were not held every Sunday; as with a lot of rural churches, our
preacher had two other churches to serve, but he would come to our
church twice a month. But whenever services were held at First Baptist all the houses on the hill were represented at least with mother
and children plus families from all around the area. Some fathers did
not quite make it to every service. We also had Sunday school and
Baptist Training Union (BTU) every Sunday. Little did I know that
these early memories of my faith began to plant the seeds in my soul
of justice and freedom for all humankind.

My father's mother, Lula Sherrod, was the superintendent of the
Sunday school, head of the deaconesses board, and church secretary.
In other words, Lula Sherrod ran the church and kept track of the
money! My grandmother was a wonderful lady. I guess she also is the
one from whom I inherited my interest in and love of cooking. She
had a large iron wood-burning stove with a large side container that
held water. When the stove was in use for cooking, it also heated the
water for daily use so we had hot water throughout the day.

I can remember my grandmother would like to take a "dip" of
snuff after dinner in the afternoon. I watched her afternoon after
afternoon, seemingly enjoying her dip so much. One day, I decided
to have a dip. Knowing where she kept her dip box, I carefully ex-
tracted some snuff from the box and tucked it in my lower lip, just
as my grandmother did. I went to sit on the front porch with her and
Miss Alice Walker, her good friend, who lived across the street. The

longer I sat the sicker I got. You talk about being sick; I thought I was going to throw up my toenails! My grandmother took me in the house and cleaned my mouth out and we then had a good talk about what adults can do but children cannot. The sickness helped me to know that there are some things little girls should not do. I really paid for that talk. To make me feel better she mixed some sugar and cocoa together and put it in my lip. I found that I did not much like this mixture either, so that experience broke up my going into her snuff box ever again.

2
Up on the Hill

Out of those nine homes on the hill there were ten children. To this day I can name them all. I can account for and know where eight of them are. The church steps were our gathering place, the grounds were our playground, and a spot under the streetlights at one corner of the church was our dreaming and planning place. We played in full view of all the adult eyes sitting on the porches of the homes up on the hill. Everybody on the hill knew everyone, all children answered to any adult, no one locked a door. Oh, how I remember those hot summer nights under the streetlight, sitting on the porch steps until our parents called us in for the night.

Two of the households I distinctly remember—the Creston Portis family and Alice Walker, who lived alone across the street from my house and who came and sat with my grandmother every afternoon, discussing the latest gossip and the problems of the day. She will never die as long as we are alive, because she would invariably say to my grandmother, "Miss Lula, I'm so full!" My grandmother would reply, "Why, what did you have for dinner, Alice?" Miss Walker would reply, listing her menu with pleasure: "Some black-eyed peas, some okra, some cornbread and some milk." To this day, after a good meal my daughter and I will quote Miss Alice: "Miss Lula, I'm so full!"

There was an ice house just down the hill that made ice for the people in the town of York. All of the people living on the hill went down daily to get ice for their ice boxes. My parents had the only refrigerator in the community. We had an ice box also, because the ice trays in the refrigerator at that time were not very large. At this time none of the hill households had indoor plumbing and people got their water from one of two wells. My grandparents had one, and the second belonged to a house that my grandparents had built and given to my father. We never stayed in that house, though, because my parents felt the "big house" needed us and it was large enough to accommodate two families. My grandparents and the three of us lived there happily for many years and water from the well was freely available to all.

My paternal grandmother, a Spelman College graduate, was the reader and writer on the hill. When the neighbors received a letter, she usually read it to them. When they needed to write a letter, she usually wrote it. She read and wrote most of the communications for all of the people on the hill.

Other memories from those days include the faces of close friends today. One of the persons has until this day remained not only a friend but, because of our closeness in York, the sister I never had. She is Margaurite Portis, whose family would live in the house with the second well, the one that had been built for my father.

The Portis family consisted of the father, Creston, his wife Miss Christine, who was one good soul God created, and their six children. Margaurite, the oldest daughter, and I would spend our days playing together at her house or mine but always within view of our parents. And play we did, making up all kinds of games to fill our days. We would tie several tin cans one after another on a long string taken from the blocks of ice that people in the community would buy each day, and then race from one line drawn in the dirt to another, and we played hop-scotch on blocks also drawn on the ground. We would also go behind the church where there was a patch of ragweed, take the weed, chop it up with a brick, roll it in some paper, and smoke it. We got caught with this one. Ball games behind the church were also a favorite pastime that could last all day. We were always together until we were called in for meals and evening baths and sometimes we even took those together! After bath time, we would gather again under the streetlight and discuss the day's events until bedtime. Because I was an only child and Margaurite was from a big family, she would often come to my house to spend the night so we could continue planning our dreams and fantasies. I can remember we would take soft drink bottles and stuff them with ice block twine. After stuffing the bottles we would wet the twine, unravel it to make it look like hair, and comb and set many different hairstyles.

Each year as the lazy summers came to an end, education became more important than play and as we began to grow, my family was faced with the dilemma of the split school session each year that Sumter County provided. When I reached school age, I was sent to live with my mother's relatives in Selma. I would always return to York for Christmas and summer to the house on the hill where my grandmother still read the community letters and the Portis family still lived. Each summer I would return home to play and share my experiences of going to school in the "big city" of Selma. While I was away how I missed Margaurite!

Later the Portis family moved from York to Mobile as their mother sought a better life for her flock as all parents did of that day. They grew up, found jobs, and began to live their lives. Time and distance kept Margaurite and me apart for some years, but the love and memories we shared would bind us together for a lifetime and the day would come when we would find each other again.

My mother, Juanita Barnett Richardson, a Tuskegee Institute and Alabama State University trained teacher, was teaching school before she and my father met and married. When we moved from Mobile to York in 1936, my mother was closer to her birthplace of Hamner, Alabama, which was only twelve miles from York. Still, I thought my mother was never really happy in York. In Mobile, she was out of the countryside and able to live in a large metropolitan city that could give her and her family more opportunities to broaden their dreams and horizons than a small town could. Yet fate declared otherwise.

3
Preparation for Life's Journey

My mother sought the best educational advantages for me and sent me away yet again, this time to live with her younger brother Harold Richardson, who lived in Washington, D.C. His wife, Norma Richardson, who was then teaching in the D.C. school system and at Howard University, was a tremendous influence in my young life. The transition from York to Selma and then on to Washington was indeed a culture shock.

So much to see and do! Aunt Norma would take me to all the government buildings and major centers. We often visited the Smithsonian and the Capitol, and even took a tour of the White House. On Sunday afternoons, we would go to the National Gallery of Art for concerts, where I developed my love for classical music. We would also go to Howard University's campus for their Lincoln programs, or to New York to see plays on Broadway. We would take the early shuttle to the city, see an opera at the Met, and return to D.C. on the evening shuttle. In York or Selma I would never have had these opportunities; young people in York knew nothing about the Smithsonian and its contents. They might have seen the Capitol in a schoolbook, but only if the white children who had used it first had not torn that page out. As with school furniture, books didn't reach black schools until white schools threw them out. Nor could they have heard a concert by the National Symphony Orchestra. It was a shock to me to know such things even existed. Just as Selma opened my eyes to life beyond York, so Washington introduced me to the greater things of the world.

My school years were spent at Banneker Junior High and Cardoza High School in Washington, D.C., wonderful schools with diverse educational programs. The schools were segregated then but far ahead of black schools in Alabama in terms of supplies, curriculum, and attitude. Students could be trained in business skills to be secretaries, clerks, and salespeople, or they could prepare to go into college after completing high school. I immediately put my feet in both fields, not really knowing if my mother could afford a college education for me on her teacher's salary, but she always told me all would work out, and as she said it would it did. While at Cardoza, I learned to type, take shorthand, and other skills I continue to utilize to this day. Both Uncle Harold and Aunt Norma were committed to expanding my horizons, and I will always be grateful for their care.

My mother had an incredible extended family. Her first cousin, Mrs. Leola Whitted, was an assistant to both the president and treasurer of Alabama State College in Montgomery. After I graduated from high school, Cousin Leola offered to take me under her wing and help me to attend Alabama State College. I enrolled there in 1950 and received my B.S. degree in secondary eduacation 1954.

While attending Alabama State under the watchful eye of Cousin Leola, I found I had to attend church with her as well. That is what all respectable young ladies did while pursuing their education, and Cousin Leola indeed kept me on the straight and narrow. When I first began my studies at Alabama State in September 1950, Rev. Vernon Johns was the minister at Dexter Avenue Baptist Church, where Cousin

Leola was a faithful member. Once again I was in the care of a strong female who was heavily involved in the work of the church, just as my grandmother and mother had been during my early years in York. My faith has always been with me from an early age. Reverend Johns had some courageous views for a black man at that time. Some time later he left Dexter for another vineyard, and in my senior year the church called as their new pastor a young minister from Atlanta, the Reverend Martin Luther King Jr.

Cousin Leola, a motherly woman with no children of her own, soon became close to the King family, especially the new pastor's wife, Coretta Scott, who was born and raised in Marion, Alabama. Cousin Leola was born in Selma, about thirty miles from Marion, and had lived there until the death of her husband, when she moved to Montgomery. In those days many families in both Selma and Marion knew each other well, given the towns' proximity. In Marion, the Scott family owned land and ran a general store. As Selma was the larger city, the Scotts went to Selma often to do business and shop for things that were not available in Marion.

Members of my mother's family, the Richardsons, had known the Scott family for years, so Cousin Leola was a familiar face to the young Mrs. King and quickly assumed a role as surrogate mother to the new family in Montgomery.

The friendship between our families and my visits to Dexter Avenue Baptist Church soon provided me with the opportunity to meet Reverend King and become reacquainted with my childhood friend Coretta. As young children we had the same music teacher in Selma, another of my aunts, Mrs. Ethel Dinkins. However, Aunt Ethel put me out of music class because she felt I had no musical ability; she only had time to work with students who showed true talent. Therefore talented Coretta stayed on, while I went on my way and to this day I cannot sing or play a note! Coretta's talent was proven when she went on to become a student at the Boston Conservatory of Music, where she met and married Martin Luther King Jr.

As often as we could, Cousin Leola and I would visit the King home on South Jackson Street in Montgomery for Sunday afternoon dinner. The fried chicken and pork and beans served in the campus dining hall were really getting tiresome. Any hot, home-cooked meal was truly a wonderful treat, especially when shared among family and friends.

After completing my course work at Alabama State in May 1954, I returned to Selma to live with my mother while looking for a job teaching as she and her two sisters were doing. It was possible to find a job in teaching or nursing during the 1950s in Alabama, but these were the only two professional occupations open to African American women, and competition was keen for the few jobs available.

One afternoon a tall, well-dressed young man came to my mother's front door in Selma, knocked, and asked, "Does Richie Jean Sherrod live here?" I replied, "Yes, I am she; may I ask who is inquiring?" He replied, "My name is Howard W. Creecy and I married Margaurite Portis of York, and I was told by my wife to find you." My face lit up like a Christmas tree, I flung the door open and began bombarding him with question after question. "Where is she? How is she? Can I go to her? Do come in!" After he entered the house another barrage of questions followed about the other members of the Portis family including sweet Miss Christine, Margaurite's mother. "Hey, slow down and let me try to answer a few of these questions," he said. I was now reconnected with my childhood sister after many years apart. Oh, happy day! After answering all my questions as best he could, we parted with his invitation for me to visit them in Dothan, Alabama, where he was pastor of First Baptist Church. Creecy, as I would come to call him over the years, would later become a prominent leader in Atlanta, where he and his family moved in the late 1950s. He became a valuable ally to Dr. King during the civil rights movement.

4
Choosing a Mate

Each summer during my student days at Alabama State, I worked in the president's office to help pay my expenses for the coming year. The summer of my junior year, 1953, I went home to Selma for the Fourth of July holiday, which was on a Saturday. On this sojourn home, as always, my family would have a picnic. On this particular outing two very good friends of the family, Dorothy and Johnny Brown, brought a friend of theirs to the picnic. Sullivan Jackson was a new dentist in Selma who had recently arrived after completing Meharry Dental School that May. We were introduced as "Dr. Sullivan Jackson, meet Miss Richie Jean Sherrod." We spoke and moved on, never a second thought on my part, though maybe somewhere in the recesses of my mind I may have thought, "He is cute, but probably married with six children." My attention turned to my family and the softball game, and when the picnic was over I went home to relax before returning to Montgomery on Monday.

The next afternoon, however, the telephone rang and the voice on the other end was Sullivan Jackson. He mentioned meeting me at the picnic and how hot it was and wondered if I would like to go for a ride for some cool air. "Oh, by the way, my sister and her husband, who I think you know, will also be along." I thought, "Why not?" as I really did not have anything to do and it was hot. I asked my mother for permission to go and because she knew his sister, she readily gave the go-ahead. He arrived with his sister Matilda and brother-in-law Evans Olds, as well as another young lady, a very good friend of mine, Mary Emma Brown, the sister of Johnny Brown, who had brought Sullivan to my family's picnic the previous day.

Later I discovered he was not married and we started dating. He would come over to Montgomery and take me out to dinner, which I greatly appreciated as another welcome break from the Alabama State food. He even brought one of my evening dresses over to Montgomery from Selma for me to wear to a campus spring dance, although my date was with another man! I graduated from Alabama State in 1954 and our lives started to change. "Sully," as I was beginning to call him, was focused on building a dental practice in Selma while I was determined to find a good job after completing college. As with many relationships in flux, problems and disagreements develop. Sully and I broke up. I decided to go on with my life, wash that man out of my hair, as the song goes.

One afternoon my dear childhood friend Margaurite came to Selma to see me and to attend a meeting with her husband. With them was a childhood friend of her husband's, Rev. Mose Pleasure Jr. Although Mose was born in Mobile, he and Howard Creecy had grown up together in New Orleans just as Margaurite and I had grown up in York. After introductions and being filled in as to who Mose was and his excellent lineage, we all went out together. Mose was working with Martin Luther King Jr. as the executive secretary of the Montgomery Improvement Association, a new organization that had been formed as a result of the Montgomery Bus Boycott. This was the struggle to be able to ride Montgomery public transit without having to stand, or sit behind white riders. This is the movement Mrs.

Rosa Parks, a black woman, generated by refusing to give up her seat and move to the back of the bus for a male white rider when she had paid the same fare to ride. On that day enough was enough for Mrs. Parks! History was made that day and many of us were aware of it.

Sully found out I had gone out with Mose Pleasure and supposedly had a heart attack! He was admitted to Good Samaritan Hospital in Selma, and his physician, Dr. William B. Dinkins, who was also my cousin, called me and asked that I come to the hospital to see him and cheer him up. The next day Sully was abruptly released from the hospital. I began to wonder if Sully had really had a heart attack or it was all an attempt to get me back. If it was, it worked! It took us some time to sort out all of the issues and realize that we really did love each other and recognize the strong desire we had to live our lives together. On March 15, 1958, Sully and I were married. Margaurite Portis Creecy was a bridesmaid in my wedding. Never again would we be further apart than a phone call.

5
The Foundation Is Laid

This house by the side of the road that has been my home for more than half a century was built in 1906 as a wedding present for my Cousin Leola and her husband, Dr. William Whitted, a dentist in Selma, by her father, Dr. Richard B. Hudson. Dr. Hudson was a well-known educator in Selma who had married my grandfather Richardson's sister, and he lived next door to his daughter's new home. Dr. Hudson was a loving father to his firstborn child, Leola, whose mother had died in childbirth. Cousin Leola and her husband moved in the new home prepared to live a happy life.

But this dream did not last long, for Leola's husband died just a few years into their marriage. Having to regroup, and with no children, she had to make some decisions; this led her to move to Montgomery to work for Alabama State College president H. C. Trenholm, who held that position for thirty-seven years until he was driven out in 1962 in retaliation for his civil rights work.

Cousin Leola leased her house to Dr. E. F. Portlock, another dentist who had recently moved to Selma, and his wife, as there was a need for a black dentist after the untimely death of Dr. Whitted. The house in Selma was again welcoming friends and relatives, and hosting civic club meetings, parties, and events for Selma's leading black citizens.

After many years of practice, Dr. Portlock's health began to fail in the early 1950s and he began to look for a young dentist to assist him. Dr. Portlock's hygienist for many years was Sully's sister, Mrs. Marie Foster. As her brother had just graduated from dental school, Marie suggested that he be invited to come down to Selma. This would be a good move, for he would be coming back to his Selma birthplace, although he had been raised since early childhood in Anderson, Indiana. Sully accepted Dr. Portlock's offer and applied for certification to practice dentistry in Alabama.

Dr. Portlock had died by the time Sully and I announced our engagement in 1957. Dr. Portlock and his wife, Benny, had been childless. Mrs. Portlock, in the house alone and knowing my family's connection to the property through Leola, invited Sully and me to live in the house with her after we were married. Later she decided to spend more time with the Portlock family in Florence, Alabama, and the house became our home, and its walls would hear the voices of people and their laughter, feel the joy and sorrow of its inhabitants, and keep the secrets of the hearts therein. So the third dentist, Dr. Sullivan Jackson, and his new bride, Richie Jean Sherrod, moved into the house by the side of the road.

Besides being a dentist, my husband was an accomplished musician on the tenor saxophone. My husband's classmates, medical and dental colleagues, musicians, and friends from his army service days were always stopping by. Some stayed overnight while others came by to get a good hot meal when passing through Selma. I enjoy cooking. It was not unusual for my husband to call to tell me somebody just phoned him or dropped by his office and that he was bringing them home for dinner. He never asked, "Do you have enough?" or "Can you prepare dinner for company?" I asked him one day, "Why do you do this to me?" His reply was, "Your cooking always tastes good to me so it should suit them as well." I knew he was proud of his home.

During the early years of our marriage, it was a sad fact that motels and hotels were not ready to accept blacks, especially in small southern towns such as Selma. When traveling, black Americans had to find lodging with family or friends or just keep going until they reached their destination. Our house by the side of the road was always open.

On occasion my husband and I would go to Montgomery, especially for the Turkey Day Classic. This is the big football game played each year between the two rival black colleges, Alabama State College and Tuskegee Institute. We would stop by to see either the King family or the Ralph Abernathy family. Ralph was from Linden, Alabama, not too far west of Selma, and was an Alabama State graduate also. He got his first practice as a demonstrator protesting the college cafeteria food, a stance with which I fully agreed. Ralph and his wife, Juanita, were then living in Montgomery, as he had taken the position of pastor of the First Baptist Church, and he became a strong ally and friend of Martin's. Juanita, who was from Uniontown, Alabama, twenty miles west of Selma, had been sent to Selma University Training School to avoid the substandard schools for blacks in smaller towns, just as I and many others had been. Juanita Jones and I were in the sixth and seventh grade together, and her parents made arrangements with yet another relative of mine, who lived just across the street from Selma University, for Juanita to be enrolled at the school. Our two families had long been friends, so there was no problem with Juanita coming to Selma—she and her parents knew people who would look after her as carefully as their own children. At one time, the whole block across the street from the school was owned by members of my family. We played up and down the same block where I now reside during those early years. We went back to our respective communities for the summers. But while we were in Selma, we played outside the house that would later become my home as an adult—the house by the side of the road. Juanita Jones finished Selma University Training School and went on to college at Tennessee State University. She met Ralph at the teacher training school, where he had also been sent by his parents for a better education.

Black families in Alabama were tight-knit; maybe we had to be to confront the hostility and discrimination society offered. If you were black and from west Alabama, people throughout the region would know you or at least your family.

A strong bond developed among the Kings, Abernathys, and Jacksons; our children were beginning to be born and we soon began to share "baby stories" to help each other along. Our own daughter Jawana was born on July 15, 1960. The men would sit back and smile at their families, and share their own hopes and dreams for the future.

There was already a relationship among the wives stemming from our childhoods in small west Alabama towns. Juanita Jones Abernathy was from Uniontown; Jean Childs (Mrs. Andrew J. Young) was from Marion, as was Coretta Scott King; and I was from York, and now lived in Selma. All of them had a standing invitation to stay with us at our home whenever they were in Selma. Plus, as my husband would always say, "My wife is a darn good cook."

6

The Port in the Storm

Several times a year all ministers from the Alabama Missionary Baptist State Convention would have meetings at Selma University, a Baptist-supported school located almost right across the street from our house. Since the school is located in central Alabama, this made it convenient for black Baptist ministers to attend meetings without having to travel long distances. Many days I would find three suitcases on our back steps with the initials R.D.A., M.L.K., and H.W.C. I knew the boys were in town and I needed to heat up the stove, get to cooking, and check the beds. The house by the side of the road is large, with three bedrooms not including the master bedroom. The men would come together or separately, Ralph and Martin from Montgomery, where they both pastored churches, and Creecy from his church in Dothan. Creecy would stop by many times, especially upon his return from visiting his family in New Orleans. We would hear singing or whistling late in the night, and my husband would turn over and say, "Creecy is here." Up we would get and the stove would be lit while he brought us up to date on news of his family.

Ralph Abernathy was from Linden in Marengo County, about fifty miles from Selma. His family consisted of many brothers and sisters, and his parents had considerable land. Juanita's family still lived in

Uniontown, only a short drive from Selma, and as they went to visit their respective families they always made a pit stop at the house by the side of the road.

My husband was a quiet, reserved man with a strength of character that stood by my side, behind me when needed, then in front of me when necessary. Sully was born in Dallas County (Selma is the county seat of Dallas), the youngest of seven children, and his mother sent him north to Anderson, Indiana, where his oldest sister was living, when he was eight years old to go to better schools and avoid the worst forms of Southern racial prejudice. Sully was eventually legally adopted by his sister, who raised him as her own with her daughter Norma Jean. Sully and Norma Jean bonded at an early age as brother and sister instead of uncle and niece, and this bond remained strong throughout their lives. After high school an uncle paid Sully's way to college and he chose West Virginia State College. Why he selected this school I never really understood and I always intended to ask him that question.

Sully went to college for two years and then was in the U.S. Army for thirty-two months during World War II, serving as a clerk with the 588th Ambulance Medical Company keeping up the medical records for our soldiers dead, wounded, or sick, and often near or even behind enemy lines. When he came home from the service he returned to West Virginia State. After completing his undergraduate studies, he was off to Meharry Medical School in Nashville, Tennessee, using the GI Bill to help finance his education.

Along the way he used his musical talents to help defray his expenses at college and at Meharry, playing with the West Virginia State Collegians Band and with the Doctors of Rhythm at Meharry. These groups were made up of experienced musicians from all over the country.

After graduation from dental school Sully joined the practice of Dr. E. F. Portlock, and continued the tradition of our home being occupied by black dentists. Sully had lived in many worlds—dental, medical, musical, and military—and was happy to have a home where his friends were welcome and found comfort. My friends and family relationships brought in the west Alabama black religious, civic, and social groups, which made us a wonderful community mosaic. The house by the side of the road became a haven for our friends from the day we moved in—especially when Sully realized his new bride could cook.

After establishing his practice, Sully attempted to cement his ties in Selma by becoming a registered voter. He was of age, a college graduate, had served his country honorably in the European theater during the war, and had secured a professional degree. But to the state of Alabama he was not considered qualified to vote. Sully had been registered in Indiana, but when he tried to transfer his registration to Alabama the answer was a resounding no. Was there a need to have a voting rights movement in this country? We all know the answer was yes, and Selma was fertile ground for this important event that would change America.

In January 1959, Sully testified before the United States Civil Rights Commission on voting rights as a means of drawing attention to this reprehensible injustice to blacks in the South and across the country. Sully and I would privately discuss this and other social problems, but little did I know a quiet groundswell was developing that would soon burst onto the world stage—with us near the center.

7
Martin Luther King Jr. the Man

How do you describe a man who was a son, brother, husband, student, scholar, theologian, orator, and author? I may have missed an adjective or two in describing Martin Luther King Jr. To this day, the question I am most often asked is, "Just what was Martin Luther King Jr. like?" Well how does a dictionary define the word "friend"? "One attached to another by affection or esteem." My husband and I felt both affection and esteem for Martin.

From 1958 until 1965 Martin was in and out of the house by the side of the road. These years after Sully and I were married really gave us time to get to know Martin the man. The four couples I have introduced to you—the Kings, Abernathys, Creecys, and Jacksons—went back and forth to visit each other during those years. These are also the years that have gone down in history—it is as simple as that. These friendships were formed by fate.

In January 1964, the Dallas County Voters League in Selma invited Dr. King, then president of the Southern Christian Leadership Conference (SCLC), to speak in Selma at Tabernacle Baptist Church, whose pastor was married to my cousin Mrs. Pauline Dinkins Anderson. Tabernacle was also the church my husband and his family attended. When Martin became a distinguished visitor in Selma and eventually known across the nation and world, we still saw him as the dear friend he was to us, not as the icon and great hope for the masses he would become. Maybe this is why he felt so comfortable around us. There was no pressure, no demands. He could relax and be at home away from home. He could and would walk around the house in my husband's pajamas and socks. Of all the times he was in the house and out of his shoes, I never saw his feet—he always wore his socks. I don't know if he slept in them or not. I often thought that maybe he did not like his feet!

Through the years Martin slept in all of the bedrooms in our house and napped on chairs, couches—anything comfortable. There was a running joke in the house about the bathrooms. Whenever Martin was about to head to the bathroom, everyone knew it would be occupied for some time, so anyone needing to go should go now or hold your peace! Shaving took time for Martin also. During this exercise, he would shave, bathe, read, and do some thinking. Ralph Abernathy was just as bad or worse. If you found both bathrooms occupied by Martin and Ralph everyone else in the house could forget it!

Martin would always tell me, "Jean, you will go down in history for being a great cook." I guess I could get his eggs just the way he liked them—the whites well done and the yellow soft, the bacon crisp. Another reason he may have liked my cooking is because none of my biscuits came out of the can. I made them from scratch as I still do to this day. During those days often I would cook around the clock and many times I had to have the stove going all day to feed the many people traveling with Martin who were in the house. It was never a problem for me, as I have always loved to cook and take pleasure in seeing those who eat my cooking enjoy it.

Martin Luther King Jr. did not like to eat a heavy meal before he addressed a mass meeting or gave a sermon. He would always eat afterward, and though the meals I served were a bit heavy for late in the evening, that's what he wanted to eat. I suppose he had built up an appetite by then and may have needed the energy for staff meetings he would then hold to review the day's activities and plan for the next day.

I tried to attend as many of the public meetings held in Selma as I could, but sometimes it became a problem. You must understand that if Martin was in town, our house was a hub of activity. There were always reporters, movement staff, and others who wanted to meet or just see the icon staying at the house by the side of the road.

We knew a white couple, friends of ours whose names are similar to ours. His name is Ira Sullivan and his wife's name is Jean Sullivan. During the movement days, some people would get confused and call the Sullivan home looking for or asking to speak to Dr. King. Jean Sullivan would respond, "This is Jean Sullivan. I think you are looking for Dr. Sullivan Jackson or his wife, Jean Jackson," and give them our number. The Sullivans as well as other white citizens in Selma were well aware that Dr. King was a regular guest in our home—this was no secret. Whenever Jean Sullivan called me, she would joke, "I know King is back in town because my phone is ringing all the time." We knew that the white folks had to live with other white folks, and they also knew their place in the town's structure. Whites had mortgages, bills to pay, and money to borrow. If they expressed a favorable opinion about the civil rights movement, they would feel pressure from their family and associates, be jeered at as "nigger lovers," or be entirely ostracized. So those who felt the movement was just and necessary stayed at home and kept their mouths closed. We knew there was some silent support for us among whites; money would be sent to us with no note, and no return address. A few would tell us, "If I was in your place, I'd be out there [demonstrating] also." Fear and peer pressure affect all of us, no matter the color. Even the churches, black and white alike.

There were also those who hated, the KKK and White Citizens Council crowd; we knew who some were and suspected others, but we certainly never asked.

The Sullivans were in an unusual situation; they could be open and friendly with blacks as they did business in the Negro neighborhood, including owning a gas station that gave credit and made small loans. So they were somewhat protected from white hostility. Over the years this contact brought about by the similarity in our names brought Jean and me together as friends, and we would later talk about the days of the movement and how much the actions in Selma have benefited the entire world.

I am very proud of my home, the house by the side of the road. For you see my home represents me—especially the kitchen. What comes out of my kitchen really represents me so I take pride in my cooking. We have always tried to make those who come into our home as comfortable as possible whether they are friends, classmates, family, or strangers, and over the years there have been many of each category. We tried hard to provide a loving environment and a peaceful haven for those who visited here, as well as for each other. To put it another way, where there is love, love is felt. Where comfort is, comfort is felt. Where respect is, respect is given in return.

I remember after Martin's long convalescence from his stabbing in New York in 1958 at a book signing party, he came to visit. After changing into his pajamas, he came into the kitchen to show Sully and me his scar. His fingers outlined the scar and he remarked, "See, if the doctor had carried the stitches another inch, I would have a perfect cross!" I ran my fingers over the scar and asked if he still had any pain. To this he remarked, "I am real careful if I have to cough!" and broke out in laughter. He was at peace with the incident and realized the lady who had stabbed him was mentally ill.

I think Martin knew from early on, while in Montgomery leading the campaign for justices on the buses, that his life was at risk. Not only was he concerned about the safety of his own family and himself, he was also keenly concerned for our safety when he was in Selma. But somewhere along the way one has to come to grips with fear. Are you going to let fear rule you? Once you make up in your mind what your course of action in life is and what the value of the cause is, then fear must take a back seat. There are too many injustices in the world to be scared of any man. This is what Martin Luther King Jr. believed in his soul.

As I mentioned, my husband twice tried in vain to register to vote and had testified before the Civil Rights Commission. After his testimony, I lost my job as an office administrator at the Selma Housing Authority. The white power elite began to look for a way to get back at Sully for testifying so they looked at me. They claimed I had spoken disrespectfully to one of the authority's board members over the phone and of course the alleged phone call never happened. The head of the Housing Authority came down to my office to tell me that I was fired but wouldn't tell me which board member I was supposed to have insulted. The office manager, who was black, said he hadn't heard such a call, but if the boss said it happened, well then it happened. He wasn't about to risk losing his job to defend me. That's just the way it was: you could stay angry and let it ruin your days, or you could move on. Sully thought he was safe from such retaliation because he was his own boss, but he was wrong. Shortly thereafter the city canceled his contract to provide dental care to city prisoners, although his office was across the street from the city jail. No reason given. This happened long before the movement even came to Selma. This should answer the question, "Did we have any reason to support the American civil rights movement?"

Both my husband and I have college educations and beyond, and despite Sully's having served his country in the military, and carrying out our basic civic responsibilities by obeying the law and paying our taxes, we still felt like second-class citizens in the country of our birth. Remember the Revolutionary War, where American patriots fought against taxation without representation? And what about the next generation?

The country asked black people like Sully to serve in the military, to give their lives if need be to protect the sacred freedoms of this country, yet some of those native citizens weren't permitted to share fully and freely in those freedoms. In a hospital emergency room you will take my blood and ask no questions if it is needed to save your life. But you don't see me as an equal, even with my heart's blood pumping in your veins. You take my tax dollars and say I have no right to say how they can be used. You take my labor and pay me less than my counterpart gets, then you ask why there is unrest from your black neighbors?

8
Storm Clouds Roll over Selma

The Dallas County Voters League invited Dr. King to speak at the annual Emancipation Service in Selma on January 2, 1965. Only a handful of blacks in Selma and Dallas County were registered voters and the Dallas County Voters League wanted to change that. They set up classes to teach blacks how to fill out application forms and how to prepare to go to the registrar's office. They encouraged people to become involved and provided transportation. I had known the organization's president, Rev. F. D. Reese, since my undergraduate days at Alabama State College. After graduation, he came back to Selma to pursue his career as a teacher and minister. We all knew his strong convictions and revulsion at being treated as a second-class citizen. For him to emerge as a local leader was not strange to me.

There had been efforts made to get more blacks registered in Dallas and the surrounding Alabama counties for some time with the involvement of the Student Nonviolent Coordinating Committee (SNCC), but it had not garnered much success. Mindful of the success the SCLC was having in Montgomery, Birmingham, and other areas, Reverend Reese and others began thinking SCLC could make a difference in and around Selma. One of SCLC's staff, the Reverend C. T. Vivian, met with the Dallas County Voters League and was impressed with the members' passion and determination. He carried this impression back to SCLC's headquarters in Atlanta and the decision was made to mount a voters' rights campaign in Selma. The Selma movement had now begun.

Reverend Reese was always a vital part of the "Selma movement," as it would come to be known. He was never officially on the staff of SCLC but he was in on countless discussions and decisions while attending the many strategy sessions at our home. I wonder if even he knows how many marches he participated in or led. He should be very proud of his ability to mobilize the Selma schoolteachers to march as a group. If people hadn't believed in the cause and trusted his leadership abilities, the famous Selma to Montgomery march would never have happened. When he and other leaders were able to get the support of the black schoolteachers, and when the white officials saw that most if not all of the black teachers, who had all been hired and could be fired at any time for any reason by the City of Selma, marching as a group, they had to begin to understand that the movement might succeed after all. As we have learned throughout history, there is strength in numbers.

9
Hosting a Movement

Dr. King accepted the invitation by the Dallas County Voters League and with the speech he gave, the Selma Movement was officially born. We had a leader. From then on Martin stayed in our home regularly when he was in town. I know of only two instances when he did not stay at the house by the side of the road. The first was when we were out of town and we made arrangements for him to stay with my aunt and uncle, Mr. and Mrs. Fred D. Williams. The other time he stayed at the Torch Motel. His stay at the Torch was decided after word had come that a credible threat had been made on his life, so he let it be known that he had changed his base of operations. This was to protect us and to confuse those who were looking to hurt him.

We had heard about the problems Martin had with the FBI, but we never pressed him for details or discussed whether the whispered accusations were true. As far as Sully and I were concerned, our friendship was built on our personal ties with Martin and Coretta, Juanita and Ralph. We knew about the wiretaps and letters, but our definition of friendship is if you are there for your friends during good times, then you must be there for them during the bad times. Who are any of us to judge each other? True or not, the whispered slander was none of our business. Our support was for the men and women who were seeking justice for all. Sometimes support meant a pat on the back, a warm smile, a cup of coffee. Our friends knew we were there for them.

I have been asked if I kept a visitor's log with the names of all those who came into our house during the days and months leading up to the march. I did not, thinking during those days that the people visiting the house by the side of the road were there on a special mission. The movement was serious business, not a social gathering. Can you see me asking John Doar, assistant attorney general of the United States Civil Rights Division, or United Autoworkers president Walter Reuther to sign my guest book?

I remember well the day John Doar came. Everyone who came to our home always went to the back door. I heard the noise of a lot of people arriving at the back door, and I went to see who they were. There were Doar and his entourage, and as he was coming on into my home, I stood in his way and asked, "Who are you? Can I help you?" Did he tell me! His stance, body language, and persona were dead serious: "I am here to see Dr. King."

"Dr. King is not out of bed yet, but you may have a seat and wait." Doar then came in with an attitude that proclaimed, "I am the U.S. government, now listen up." Later, I remember thinking to myself that the federal government now no longer uses the phone; they just show up and completely take over. I sat them around the dining room table and I went to tell Martin of their arrival. Martin joined them in a few minutes still in his (actually my husband's) pajamas.

Doar's tone in talking to Martin was emphatic. "Do you realize the repercussions this march will have? We know what you are planning, and you're going too fast. These problems with voter registration are on the agenda, we'll get to them." Martin, who knew exactly who had sent him and why, listened and then responded in a normal but firm tone: "We're sorry to disagree, but we are going forward with our plans." Martin then stood up, thanked Mr. Doar for coming to see him, and walked out, as dignified as a man in pajamas could ever be. When Doar and his men left, their attitude had changed from aggressive confidence to those of men who have to give their boss bad news.

When these meetings took place I would fade into the woodwork, continuing to cook, tidy and clean up, and be as normal as possible and, as I wasn't staff, not hearing or seeing what went on, yet hearing and seeing everything. I very seldom gave my opinion unless I was asked.

I could always tell when President Lyndon Johnson was calling our home. The phone would ring, usually late at night, and when I would answer a voice on the other end would say, "This is the White House operator calling for Dr. Martin Luther King Jr." I would quickly find Martin, tell him that President Johnson was calling, and connect a phone near him if one was not already in his room. I would make sure he was not disturbed, moving away and closing all doors behind me. I would also tell others in the house who Martin was talking to. He and the president would talk for a long time. Martin told me sometimes the calls would last so long that he would fall asleep, then wake up, and the president would still be talking.

I never asked about these conversations. President Johnson seemed to know when Martin was in the house. I used to wonder about that. Sometimes he would have just arrived in the house after a demonstration or large meeting, and the phone would ring from White House operator 1800 as Martin came in the door.

My husband and I were friends of the King family. We were not SCLC staff members. We wanted to contribute whatever we could for the greater cause. After all, we are black, Negroes, African

Americans—whatever you wish to call us. I think of myself as an American with African and other bloodlines running through my veins. I was nevertheless born in the United States of America, which makes me a citizen of this country with my own individual and particular hue! We were happy to do what we could to assist Martin and his staff in whatever way they thought the most useful.

Family and friends began to call after pictures of the house by the side of the road were seen in national magazines and newspapers. "Is this true what we are seeing and hearing about you guys?" "Yes," we would reply. "Aren't you in danger?" "Yes, but what can we do? Danger is everywhere. We are trying to be as safe as possible."

After a while we suspected that our phone was bugged. Upon picking up the receiver you could hear a click, ever so slight but it was noticeable. Sometimes when the house was quiet and if Martin or his staff were not in the house, I would call my mother or friends, and just for the heck of it would say, "I'm just talking to my family; there is no need to listen, unless you want to hear the latest town gossip!" On other occasions I would say, "Everybody has gone, there is no need to waste good tape on what I am saying."

10

Dangerous Days

We did not tell our family and friends about the threats we received, some claiming bombs or other mayhem would be directed at the house, and others threatening my husband's life. Had all these possible dangers been known by our family, Sully's mother in Indiana would have been down here in no time and the Klan would have been history. No one was going to bother her Hun, as she affectionately called Sully. We knew about fifty-three year old Mrs. Annie Lee Cooper whacking Selma sheriff Jim Clark with her purse when he displayed very bad manners by trying to shove her out of the voter registration line in the Dallas County Courthouse. Sully's mother would have made Mrs. Cooper look like a schoolgirl! On that particular day Sheriff Clark was not at his best. He was "tired of all of the niggers trying to invade his courthouse." Anger was getting the best of him. He decided to push Mrs. Cooper. He pushed the wrong lady. Mrs. Cooper immediately slammed his hand with her pocketbook. It finally took three deputies to wrestle her to the ground. Martin was standing across the street that day and witnessed the whole incident. Whenever the press knew King was in town they were all around. The press saw the Cooper incident, took photos, and wrote it up in detail.

The story was all over the evening news across the country with Jim Clark standing over Mrs. Cooper with a billy club. Not a pretty sight.

Today, Mrs. Cooper is a registered voter and still a leader in the community. How I love and respect that lady!

That Sheriff Jim Clark, bless his heart wherever he is. If his heart had not been filled with so much hate, the movement would have had some problems, but we could always count on him to give the correct amount of fuel to the fire when it was needed. He did not realize his contribution, nor did his supporters and backers. They were clueless heroes of our struggle. Their actions just added determination to Reverend King and all of us to work even harder to secure our rights, and demonstrated to anyone watching TV or reading the newspaper just what we were up against. Clark also did not realize the Justice Department was planning suits against him for denial of basic civil rights, and that the FBI was also building a file on him.

You see, when you hate, your vision is blurred and you can't see or feel the other side of the coin. You just hate. And what is the reason for hate? I think the answer lies in people's own insecurities, fears, and ignorance, and in the most powerful motivation of all—the need for power.

Reverend Abernathy once said that Jim Clark deserved to be an honorary member of the movement. The world saw him strutting around, beating and shoving marchers—unarmed, peaceful men, women, children—on the Edmund Pettus Bridge and elsewhere and for what? Once during the Selma movement, we heard that Jim Clark was very ill and had to go to the hospital. This caused the movement more stress and worry: what were we going to do without Sheriff Clark? What could we do to help him recover? We heard he had a heart attack and was in Vaughn Regional Hospital, later to find out his problem was a result of stress and fatigue. I guess for Jim Clark fighting an unjust war against other human beings was somehow wearing him down—only he did not realize this either!

The city knew that SCLC and SNCC would be coming to town, and we had been told that meetings were being held among the white leadership regarding what to do about it. Meetings were also held between white and black leaders. The city had a new mayor, Joseph T. Smitherman, who was seen at the time as a moderate. It was Smitherman who named Wilson Baker as Selma's new public safety director, and boy did we ever need one.

If Jim Clark had listened to some of the white citizens and Wilson Baker, the movement could have died on the vine in Selma. "Tell them yes to everything, sure we'll think about your issues, let's register a few blacks, make them feel good and maybe they will forget and get back to normal—then we will conduct business as usual." But wait a minute—God had put Jim Clark into the mix to show the country and the world just what kind of democracy this country really had. How can we tell others how to live, when there is dirt all over our faces as Americans, committing wrongful acts against our citizens—and at times still happening to this day!

I would hope that God saw the good in Wilson Baker's heart to let him into heaven when he died. I personally would ask for another star in his crown for he surely did look after the house by the side of the road. He and his men knew more about the underside of our house than we did. Whenever a bomb threat would come in, all we had to do was call. He and his men would check it out and make sure we were as secure as he could make us. Mr. Baker was an intelligent, educated man who was as fair as he could be living in those times and in Selma, and realizing in his soul that the movement was just and right. Mr. Baker once said, "If I were a black man I would be out there

fighting for the same rights." In the many times I saw him I never felt
hostility in him or saw hatred in his eyes. He played an integral part
in the Selma campaign and thus the American civil rights movement.
I believe much more harm and violence would have occurred if it had
not been for Wilson Baker.

Many a day and night a car would be parked out in front and in
back of the house, on the lookout for possible trouble and to keep
perpetrators from carrying out their devious plans. There would be
a rock or two thrown on the front porch, but we never had even a
window broken. What fear we felt came from the language and the
threats over the phone. We never knew if some fool would try to
throw a firebomb or some other device at the house by the side of the
road, and we know well some fool might have if Mr. Baker and his
men hadn't been nearby.

Late one afternoon, Martin was sitting in the dining room at the
head of the dining table talking with us when the phone rang. A friend
of ours, Johnny Brown, was calling to ask, "What's going on around
there? The KKK is parading in front of your house." We wanted to
jump up and get Martin to a safer part of the house and away from
the window he was sitting by, into an inner hall where he would be
out of immediate danger. Instead of moving quickly as I wanted him
to, he wanted to go into the living room and look out into the street
to see the men in their sheets and robes. We finally convinced him
that this wouldn't be too wise. The KKK made only one pass by the
house but the parade did cause our hearts to beat a little faster.

Years later Jim Clark had sunk about as low as he could: his wife
left him, his children would have nothing to do with him, he wan-
dered from state to state trying to find a job doing anything. Would
you believe years later he finally came back to Selma and asked one
of the black leaders in the movement for a job?

11

Uncle Martin

Dr. King always called my mother his "Selma mother," which she enjoyed being when he was in Selma. One day he arrived in Selma with a cold and my mother made him a potion that only mothers of those days could make: red onions, honey, lemon, and several teaspoons of whiskey. She would cook this until all was blended well and give Martin several spoonfuls. Feeling better after sleeping for awhile, he would tell her she needed to bottle this potion and sell it throughout the land!

You can imagine the changes she had seen in her lifetime. It was amazing to hear her stories and realize how she adjusted to over one hundred years of life and she was always looking forward to seeing a few more changes to adapt to!

Our daughter and only child, Jawana Virginia Jackson, was born on July 15, 1960. Finally, after all these years, the house by the side of the road would have a child to fill its walls with laughter! The birth of our daughter put a glow on the dim light that had been burning in our hearts regarding the social issues in this country and the civil rights movement.

Jawana knew Martin from the time she was born. To have him in the house was nothing unusual. To Jawana he was simply "Uncle

Martin." Being the type of person he was, and having children of his own, he gave children "special time"; even if only for a few moments, he made them feel that they had his undivided attention. He indeed had a gift for relating to children and he related quickly to Jawana.

This was her home and she had the free run of it, and later it did become a problem when Uncle Martin was in a meeting somewhere in the house and she was told that she could not disturb him. Explaining to a four-year-old why all of these people were in her home and that seeing Uncle Martin and what he was doing wasn't possible this minute was at best difficult. Very early, one of the times he was away from the house we sat with her and tried to explain Uncle Martin's important role: "Just as Daddy has a job to take care of people's teeth, Uncle Martin is trying to help people, too. By helping Uncle Martin we are helping make your life better, too."

"But Mamma, Uncle Martin is a preacher who lives in Atlanta. We went there to see him in his church. He called my name from up there where he was."

"Yes, and Uncle Martin works very hard for all of us."

Children often accept the explanations of those they trust, understanding on their level as long as you are truthful with them. I believe children have the God-given ability to look into your eyes and know if they can trust you to tell the truth.

Whenever Jawana was in the house we made sure she was introduced to whoever was there. This made her feel a part of what was going on. Even though she was very young, she needed to be included. After such introductions, she would usually go on her way continuing to play.

Sometimes we would receive a telephone bomb threat, and we needed to get her out of the house quickly. When the threats occurred, we would take Jawana over to stay with my mother (whom she called Ban Dam). Going to Ban Dam's house was no problem; she enjoyed going to see her grandmother and great-grandmother (Emma Richardson), who then lived with my mother in Selma. Both women had moved to Selma in the 1940s, my mother from York and my grandmother from Hamner. Many a night we would have to call a nearby relative or a friend that Jawana knew well to come to our back fence, which ran along a quiet alleyway, and hand her over the fence to safety covered with a blanket. As her parents, we were committed to our involvement and had placed our faith in God to take care of us, but our daughter needed to have a chance to grow up, have a future, make her own commitments, and have the productive life that had eluded many of her ancestors in this country.

Every time Uncle Martin came to the house he brought Jawana something, usually a five-dollar bill. Since Martin hardly ever carried any money on his person, he would put his hand behind his back for someone to bail him out. Usually it was Jawana's father who came to his rescue. Then he would cheerfully give our daughter the money, and that made him even more special in her young eyes! With the money he gave her on his visits, her father and I bought her U.S. savings bonds, which she still has to this day.

On one of his visits, Martin brought Jawana a newly published children's book, written by Ed Clayton, with pictures and stories about him as a child. Martin had signed the book and added a personal inscription to her that read "To Juana, my niece, for whom I wish a great future and whose parents I admire dearly, from Uncle Martin." When he presented the book to her, her small, smiling face drained when she opened the book and read the inscription. Pulling on his coattail she cried, "Uncle Martin, you have known me all of my life and Mamma said you have been to school, but you don't know how to spell my name!"

"Well, Jawana, Uncle Martin is awfully sorry. How do you spell your name?" She slowly spelled her name to him. On one of his next visits, a new copy of the book was presented to her from Uncle Martin with the correct spelling of her name.

I can remember once Martin came to Selma with a very bad cold and not feeling well at all. Jawana also had a cold when Martin arrived. I put Jawana in her bed and Martin in bed in another room. Not having any of my mother's potion on hand, I gave each some cough syrup that we called "Jawana's make me feel better medicine." Later, thinking both were resting, I went to check on Martin and to my surprise I heard Jawana say, "Mamma, Uncle Martin and I are sick." She had left her bed and climbed in with Martin, and he was reading her a story from one of her books. She finally did go to sleep and we carried Jawana back to own room and bed. Sometime later in the night, Martin tried to give himself some cough medicine, dropping spoon and medicine on the carpet, and then in trying to clean it up made a bigger mess. I finally heard him and tried to make little of the incident to keep him from feeling any worse than he already did. The spot remained in the house for years until we finally had the carpet replaced in that room many years later. I called it "Martin's feel better medicine spot."

After growing up and finishing high school, Jawana decided to attend Fisk University in Nashville, Tennessee. Upon entering Fisk at the age of sixteen, our daughter had led a life up to that point that had certainly been interesting. Her years spent at Fisk would prepare her for adulthood and expose her to many more characters on the stage of life. I have mentioned my belief that the threads of life bind us all together. Jawana's threads would soon begin to make her own mosaic that would include many threads from our lives as well.

After successfully completing undergraduate and graduate studies at Fisk, she decided to live in Atlanta. Off our daughter went to Atlanta to start her life! Sully and I had supported our precious daughter throughout the years and in all the hopes we still had for her. After all, wasn't Jawana and the hope we had for her success the reason we supported Martin and the American civil rights movement?

Howard and Margaurite Creecy had moved to Atlanta in the early 1960s, and Jawana's first home in Atlanta would be with them. Our wish was that Jawana would have more opportunities in Atlanta to spread her wings and fly higher than we ever could.

Later Jawana worked with Coretta Scott King at the King Center in Atlanta, where she spent ten years on staff. During these years Jawana found herself having to address "Aunt Coretta" as "Mrs. King" and sometimes found herself slipping even in public settings! Jawana believes that her years working at the King Center were part of her life's plan and an opportunity to contribute to the work of Uncle Martin and the civil rights movement. While at the center she had a unique opportunity to meet and work with a host of dignitaries and heads of state from all over the world, many of whom were seeking to continue the work of Martin Luther King Jr. after his death. Her work at the center also enabled her to develop her public speaking skills and to advance her natural writing skills.

I am so proud of her and the lady she has become. She has given of herself and used her abilities to make this a better world. Her father and I realized that we had indeed made the right decision early in her life: to support justice and social freedom for all. What more can parents ask for?

12

Shelter for the Spirit

As the Selma movement gained momentum and the dangers to Martin became more intense, Bernard Lee started traveling with him, which meant he came to the house more often. There was a great need to monitor calls, visitors, and reporters trying to see or talk to Martin Luther King Jr. Bernard handled much of this because some of the faces I did not know and many of their questions I could not answer.

Bernard was like another member of the household. He knew where everything was and became another set of hands for me and ears for Martin. I believe Bernard was loyal to Martin and the goals of the movement. Martin Luther King Jr. was truly his leader. I don't know where Bernard was born or when he joined SCLC. One day he just showed up with Martin and began to coordinate his daily activities and travel with him, and became another set of eyes. Slender in stature and quiet, Bernard was another product of Alabama State University in Montgomery. He would take phone calls, relay the messages, decide who could see Martin and who could not. Bernard would gather and pack his clothes, and make sure his travel was done on time. Bernard really took some of the pressure off of me as it pertained to Martin's personal matters. He was a real jewel of the movement.

Many times Bernard's hands and those of Andrew J. Young had to be spanked for passing by the stove and eating the bacon or whatever I was cooking to put on the table. Bernard was a joy to have in the house not only for his respect for "his leader" but also for his ability to defuse tension. When faced with two people who did not see eye to eye on a particular subject, he would simply shuffle one into one room and the other into another room so that neither would come into contact with the other until peace could be restored.

Having someone skilled at handling the reporters became crucial, because I did not realize there were so many on the planet! During the days Martin was staying with us, reporters would use any ruse to get in. They set up tripods for cameras in the front yard, in the backyard, and on our porch to take pictures of who came and went. Some I would know because I had seen them on television; many I did not know. The importance of having reporters on the scene was demonstrated clearly by the tragic events of February 18, 1965, that awful night Jimmy Lee Jackson (no family relation to us) was shot in Marion, Alabama.

Any mass meeting held at night was dangerous. There were many discussions about whether to have night marches. The possibility was always voted down because of the inability to control the situation and to know what threats might be lurking in the darkness. Those who spoke in favor of night marches wanted the advantage of numbers, as night meetings and marches could potentially draw more people as they would be off work then, and able to attend. But the voices urging caution always won out.

In Marion I don't think there was a plan for a march that night. It just happened. Marion is a small town off the beaten track, and there had been demonstrations and arrests there for several weeks. On February 18 James Orange, an SCLC leader from Birmingham who was coordinating the protests there with local leaders, was arrested. Black protestors meeting in Mount Zion Baptist Church were addressed by Rev. C. T. Vivian, and the idea for a march came out of raw emotion. C. T. could bring emotion to a fever pitch to any group he spoke to. A large group then decided to march to the Perry County jail to protest Orange's arrest. The meeting leaders knew that the State Highway Patrol and local law enforcement officers were outside the church and thought they would provide a certain amount of protection for the marchers. They were dreadfully wrong. It was February and dark came fast. Somebody cut off the streetlights, and state troopers and local police attacked the crowd.

After the lights went out in downtown Marion it became a free-for-all and a very dangerous situation. The marchers began to scatter. Viola Jackson, mother of Jimmy Lee, was in the Mount Zion Baptist Church that night and marched down the public streets where she paid taxes, and probably expected law enforcement, whose salaries her tax dollars helped to pay, to protect her. Jimmy Lee Jackson moved to protect his mother from the whirling billy clubs and cattle prods. Shooting began and he was in harm's way. Jimmy Lee Jackson was mortally wounded, and five other marchers and three reporters were badly beaten.

The cover of darkness always seems to have a strange effect on some people. Their darker side comes out. I always did wonder who cut off the streetlights that night. Then again, when all are of one accord they work together. Maybe the attackers also figured, who would care or would notice activity in a small rural town like Marion? Were the reporters singled out for attack? Probably. They were white, and the attackers didn't like that, whites marching with Negroes, and if they did realize they were reporters they probably didn't like that either. One such reporter was Richard Valeriani of NBC. Movement leaders liked and trusted him because of his fair reporting and his continuous presence wherever the action was, and he was one of the reporters who was severely beaten. Valeriani, along with Jimmy Lee Jackson and the others who were injured, had to be brought to Selma to the hospital. What the reporters saw that night the cameras recorded. News accounts of that night were on the morning news the next day with all of the gruesome details. Movement leaders in Marion that night made their way out of the sea of people in downtown Marion and came back to the house by the side of the road in Selma. We spent that night washing bloody shirts, attending to bruises and cuts, and dealing with disappointment along with the fear that followed.

The staff was lead by C. T. Vivian because Martin was not in Selma that night. Vivian phoned Martin as soon as his group reached our house and they all went into an immediate strategy session to determine the next step. There were decisions to be made about how the events of the night could be turned to a good purpose and used to reveal the depth of the hatred and lawlessness we faced. People were going in and out of the house, keeping track of those taken to the hospital. Strange cars began to circle the block. A report then reached the house that C. T. Vivian was in danger, and it was necessary to get him away as soon as possible. It was time for Jawana to go over the back fence and off to her Ban Dam's.

Reporters began showing up from everywhere, partly because some of their own had been injured and partly because of the sheer magnitude of the violence that night. In fact, one would think the reporters were coming up from the ground! The telephone began to ring off the hook. News came in and went out. Who can carry a message? Watch the windows, stay by the doors.

Who is going to take C. T. to the Montgomery airport and when can he catch a plane out? We finally talked an off-duty black police officer who lived around the corner from us to drive him to Montgomery. If he could secretly be sent out and only a few of us knew when or where, the others could honestly say they didn't know where he was. C. T. and his driver decided since it was late at night they should not travel the usual U.S. Highway 80 route but go the back way along Alabama Highway 14 to Montgomery. In Montgomery there were safe houses known only to a few and he could get on a plane early the next morning. It's the middle of February, the dead of winter. In his rush to get out of Marion, C. T. had left his overcoat behind. So C. T. went over the back fence in my husband's overcoat. Sully never saw that coat again!

That night fear did creep into my mind; as a matter of fact it came in as thick as mud. And I wasn't alone. Confusion bred fear, as it wasn't clear at first who had attacked the marchers at Marion, although we knew at least some police had been involved. Would they follow the staff back to Selma and continue their attacks? Will a fire-bomb come through the window? Then I spoke to my fear and said, I have hurt people to tend to, tired people who need food and rest, coffee to make, sandwiches to fix, and the ever-ringing phone to deal with. "Hey, someone talk to that reporter and can I get through this room please? Did someone check with the hospital to see how the injured are doing? Mr. Valeriani was hurt—will he make it?" Many of the staff knew he had been beaten over the head pretty badly. Will morning ever come? So as I moved from washer to dryer, from tub to sink, from refrigerator to stove, I drew strength from my work and from my husband, who was a rock of quiet strength. "Do what you can, Bay [his pet name for me], everything will work out."

Observing C. T. Vivian taught me a lot about dealing with fear. He always seemed to elude fear. In the most difficult situations, such

as dealing with Jim Clark on the steps of the Dallas County Courthouse with deputies, billy clubs, guns, and cattle prods, he always
spoke with a quiet, firm voice. His face told you he really believed in
what he was doing and was using his considerable intellect to analyze
the situation, all while somehow never being afraid.

13
Our Neighborhood

Our neighborhood is made up of older, educated, settled persons. Selma University is close by, and a number of our neighbors were senior faculty and staff there. My husband and I were the youngest couple on the street for several blocks. The neighbors saw all of the people and cars coming and going, the KKK marching by, and the reporters setting up shop on our porch and in the yard. I knew our neighbors were nervous about all the activity on our street but they stayed quiet for the most part. However, had I asked for help from any neighbor I am sure in my heart that many if not all of them would have heard my call. The Smiths, who lived next door and shared a driveway with us, never said a word about the crowded driveway or the throngs of reporters that would surround the house. In fact, they let me store canned goods at their house because I ran out of storage space in my kitchen. As a result of being next door to our house, the Smiths found that their phone was cut off or had "trouble on the line." Through it all they never complained and for that I am always grateful.

Outside of our immediate block, there were many who made their quiet contributions. Some took out-of-town student and adult demonstrators into their homes, feeding and sheltering them at their own cost. Sometimes their own children would sleep on the couch or on the floor. Many, including some of my neighbors, would go to the movement headquarters church to clean up, to help in the kitchen, or whatever needed to be done to support the mass meetings. There were indeed a lot of unsung heroes in Selma working behind the scenes throughout the struggle. I remember one lady who lived near one of the major churches in Selma saying she could not march because of trouble with her legs. But she quickly offered to help the young students who were in town with the movement wash their clothes. Many other contributions we will never know.

Others we had known as friends became very quiet and invisible. Fear worked on some; they worried they might get caught in the middle if the house were attacked, or that being seen with us might harm their livelihood. Others would say, "I'm behind you," and we didn't see them again because that was exactly where they were. Surprising as it may sound, there were others who somehow didn't realize what was going on. What demonstrations?

People and reporters were constantly around the house, asking to see Martin to talk to him about this and that, or just to touch the hem of his garment, and usually they had their own agenda. For a reporter, to get one interview with King over their byline would sure help their career. In this atmosphere of crowds of people wanting to get close to Martin to further their own needs, one day a local Roman Catholic priest, Father Maurice Ouellet, came by the house. My husband, who knew the priest very well, took him to see Martin. Being the gracious person that he was, Martin listened to the priest and had a friendly but short conversation. Pleased and satisfied, the priest thanked Martin and my husband, and then left.

Later that day Martin said to Sully in a very quiet manner, "I see you are making appointments for me now instead of fixing teeth. I thought you were my friend." In his way he was telling Sully not to bring people to see him without his knowing about it. We got the point loud and clear. But later that same day, as a result of the earlier conversation, Father Ouellet returned, bringing a large contribution of money for the movement, gave it to Martin, and pledged his support for our cause. Sully said, "Sometimes things happen for a reason," and Martin understood loud and clear.

Something we understand now was that it was important for Father Ouellet as well. I visited him not long ago, just before finishing this book, and he still spoke with emotion of his sense that he had been in the presence of a truly extraordinary man, and he reminded me that Martin had invited him to stand with him and the other ministers at the funeral of Jimmy Lee Jackson. He quoted several lines of Martin's sermon to me, without notes, after more than forty years. Sully was right—sometimes things do happen for a reason, even if we don't undertsand the far reaching effect an action can have until later.

14
Guests in the House

On February 1, 1965, Martin led a group of over 250 demonstrators to the Dallas County Courthouse in an attempt to register to vote, only to be all arrested, including Martin, by Sheriff Clark for "parading without a permit." The sheriff was beginning to get excited and nervous; perhaps those he answered to were beginning to feel uncomfortable with the steady unfavorable national and international attention Selma was getting, or perhaps Clark himself thought he could end the demonstrations and voter drive with harsh treatment. A few days later he arrested more than 150 other marchers, mostly high school students, and as the county jail was already full, Clark and his deputies forced the youngsters to run to the National Guard armory outside town where they were to be held. We didn't know it yet but Clark and other law enforcement officials were beginning to get desperate and even a bit panicked by the demonstrations, which weren't ending; indeed, they were growing. The violent overreactions of Jim Clark and people like him who didn't know what to do when Negroes clearly were no longer ruled by fear would soon result in the beginning of the end for the whole system Clark was desperately trying to save. If so many people hadn't gotten hurt and some even killed, it might be funny to think Jim Clark was probably doing as much as Martin Luther King to end segregation and second-class citizenship!

We hadn't expected that Martin was going to jail, but once we found out he was indeed there, tension mounted. How he would be treated in the Selma jail was our number one concern. Yet Martin was skilled at turning his arrest to the movement's advantage; a few days later his "letter from the Selma jail" was in the *New York Times,* pointing out that there were more Negroes in jail with him than were on the voting rolls in the whole county. That same day Martin was released; I don't know who pushed whom, but it's my guess Clark was told to let him go.

The day before he was released Martin called me from jail and asked if I would prepare a luncheon for forty congressmen.

"Who?" I said.

"I have invited congressmen to come to the house and talk and see for themselves the need for this movement, and to garner their support. This may give our cause some visibility," he replied.

"Martin, do you mean United States congressmen?"

"You can do it; just cook for us, do your usual thing."

"When?"

"Tomorrow, February 5. I know this is short notice but I also know you can do it!"

After I hung up and caught my breath, all sorts of problems and questions presented themselves. We were boycotting the white grocery stores in town, so now where do I get food? I need to get out the good china and the silver needs cleaning. We can't serve this group on paper plates! Some serious dust needs to be pushed out of the way. How am I going to get all of this done? Forty plates? Where do I get forty plates and sets of table silver? After going to get Mamma's set of twelve and checking with all my aunts, yes, I decided, I could probably produce forty plates and I already had silver coming out of my ears! After all, I had inherited a few pieces over the years. Pull it all together and it will be enough.

I didn't have an industrial stove for all of the cooking that was done during January through March 1965, just a regular four-top burner stove found in all households. My stove did get a workout from morning through the day and far into the night.

The main ingredient for cooking is organization. Start by deciding what you are preparing. Make sure you have what it takes to make all the dishes you will serve. Start with one dish, put it together, and clean up as you go along, putting away used items when finished with them. Never start two or three dishes at the same time. Your kitchen should be clean and ready for a new preparation at all times. Prepare as much as you can ahead of time and put dishes into the refrigerator or freezer. My refrigerator is regular size, but I also had a full upright freezer, which really came in handy. Foods such as collard greens, macaroni and cheese, rice, and so forth can be cooked ahead of time and frozen to be used later. Did you know everything can be safely frozen except eggs and white potatoes?

Dr. King and his staff were never in the house for long periods of time but were in and out often. Between sessions, I had the opportunity to restock the kitchen, clean the rest of the house, and reorganize for the next event.

Finally, I had a quiet moment with myself about this dinner. "This is no different from any other person or persons you have cooked for. Calm yourself and do what has to be done." On a day-to-day basis I did not have any help in the house even though I could have used it because of the sheer number of people who were living here. My husband and I did not want any information leaking out from the house. We could control what we said or did but we could not control the actions of others. But for this special occasion, I did seek some help simply because I could not pull this one off alone in such a short period of time. I called a lady I knew, Mrs. Minnie White, and asked her to help. She was a person I could leave in the house with complete trust and who would do what was needed to be done. While she was moving dust, I went to Uniontown, about twenty-five miles west of Selma, to shop for food. I did not want to serve rubber chicken to this group. What could I serve that could be prepared ahead of time but still be fresh and good? Remember, my motto is that anything coming out of my kitchen represents me, and I still love to cook for groups to this day. Soon, all of the dust had been moved. Tables were set, and would you believe it, I did fix chicken—just another way, more like chicken à la king with my own style of rice pilaf and a hot fruit dish. The menu also included hot homemade rolls made by another friend, coffee, and iced and hot tea. Forty U.S. congressmen had been expected, but only fifteen showed up for lunch that day although some were accompanied by their aides.

I asked another friend of mine, Dorothy (Dot) Brown, to come and help me serve on the day of the event. Happily, she agreed despite being very much pregnant. I remember after the crowd thinned out, Dot asked Martin to bless and pray for the unborn baby. He smiled and put his hand on her stomach and said a prayer. He prayed for her to deliver a healthy baby and for her labor to be easy. She and I have laughed about that over the years.

After the congressmen left, a full-scale staff meeting was called to evaluate and plan future strategy. Staff once again was coming and going, phone calls were made to New York, Washington, Los Angeles— on and on it seemed to go. I was so tired I remember crawling into a corner just to let the world pass me by for a little while. Later that afternoon, Martin left for New York and then home to Atlanta to get some rest and peace after having been in jail for several days. He hadn't been particularly mistreated—the jailers knew everyone's attention was on them—but jail is no place to rest.

Looking back, I realize how strange it all was: this man, Martin, in a way just a black preacher, thrown into a southern jail, where he plans a lunch for a large group of U.S. congressmen, then after he is let out a few days later he is on his way up to a Washington meeting with the president over voting rights!

Martin Luther King Jr. was to so many people just a few steps below Jesus Christ. If Martin Luther King could not do it, then there was only one other place to go: God himself. The acceptance, the belief, the trust was so great in this one man. Martin Luther King Jr. could have asked people to walk on water and they would have tried. The weight of this trust and faith is what I believe placed a heavy burden on Martin and was the cause of the depression that hit him from time to time. Like everyone, he had times of self-doubt. What if he could not deliver what people expected? What if the movement did not succeed? The pressures and fears my husband and I felt seemed great to us but compared to Martin's they were miniscule.

15
Other Voices in the House

When Dr. Benjamin E. Mays, the longtime distinguished president of Morehouse College in Atlanta, walked into the house I almost felt like standing and placing my hand over my heart just out of great respect for this dynamic man. Dr. Mays came to the house by the side of the road mainly, I felt, to give his moral support to one of his most famous students. Talking in private with him, with no staff present, I am sure Martin Luther King Jr. appreciated his coming and welcomed his wisdom.

Our daughter, Jawana, bless her heart, never met a stranger. Meeting Dr. Mays with Uncle Martin, and Martin's explanation that this man was a teacher, impressed her. Dr. Mays, being the educator that he was at heart, paid attention to the questions she asked. It became clear that both he and Martin were interested in her abilities and possible future.

Dr. Mays asked me if she was in a preschool program for gifted children. I explained we didn't have such programs in Selma. Then I asked him what had he seen in her that made him think she needed a special school. His reply was that she needed to be tested to determine her IQ. He felt those results would help her father and me make decisions about her education. He even set up the appointment for her to be tested at Atlanta University with an evaluator he knew. Here again, if only the walls could talk! What a joy it was to have this great educator and scholar eating a meal at the house by the side of the road.

We made the trip to Atlanta for the test with Jawana, who was now five years old. She enjoyed playing games with the "nice man" in a big room. We were pleased with the results. While in Atlanta, we stayed with Juanita and Ralph Abernathy. Their children were also young. This trip also resulted in Jawana's first date. Little Ralph, their oldest son, invited Jawana to the movies to see *The Sound of Music*. Juanita told him that we all might like to see the movie so off we all went.

One staff member you always knew was in the house from the moment his foot hit the first step was Hosea Williams. The minute you heard "My leader!" you knew Hosea was somewhere around Martin. He would give his report of what was going on "in the street" and at the churches. We called him the "Street Lieutenant." One thing is for certain: Hosea had very strong opinions and those in charge always knew how he felt and what he believed should be done. Hosea would argue a point until the cows came home. Voices would get loud, usually those of James Bevel, James Orange, and Hosea. Dr. King would just listen, and after all views had been expressed the matter would then go to a higher level. There would be more discussion among Martin, Ralph Abernathy, and Andrew Young, still in the same room or in another room, and then finally one of the top three would announce the final decision.

There were times when Hosea would be given a directive or plan not to his liking and he would abruptly leave. Then he would do exactly what he wanted to do in the first place. Later at another staff meeting he would say, "I told you what would work," and most times it did.

Hosea had a true feel for the streets. He knew the attitude of the ordinary person out on the street and had the ability to get people to do what was necessary. To see him work a crowd was fascinating: he looked like everyone else, always wearing overalls. Indeed, when he was really dressed up he just added a white shirt and tie with a denim jacket to the overalls.

Hosea never, as far as I can remember, really spent the night in the house by the side of the road, but he took many, many naps on the floor when he was worn out from activity or arguing. There was a standing instruction when he dozed off: "Don't wake Hosea up. Let him sleep!"

Sully came home from his office one afternoon to find throngs of people, reporters, and onlookers in front of the house as he was attempting to get up the driveway. He was told by a man watching the back door, "You can't go in there. Dr. King is in there and about to have a news conference." Sully smiled and responded, "Is the lady of the house in there?" The man said she was. "Well, then, if I don't get in there for my dinner she is going to be very upset." The man then realized this might not be just another visitor and asked, "Do you live here? Are you Dr. Jackson?" Sully told him he was, and the man said, "Then you can go in." Sully smiled and thanked him, and joined the crowd inside.

He came in the house very amused, telling Martin he could not get into his own house. We realized that a better system might be needed, and the staff asked us to make a list of those likely to come by and who should be allowed in the house. My mother and Sully's sisters went on the list and I added a friend of mine, Louise Mitchell, a schoolteacher, counselor, and test coordinator for the Dallas

County school system. During the movement Louise saw students come to school, check in as being present, and then walk out as had been preplanned. Teachers knew where the students were going and why. Since the teachers were at work they could not join the protests during the day for fear of losing their jobs, but once the students had checked in and been recorded as present, they could leave and not be listed as absent from school; then they could do whatever they wanted without fear of punishment. And what most wanted was to join the group protesting at the courthouse or rallying in a church. When Louise came by, she was my news source for what was going on out in the town, as I was busy most days looking after the throngs of hungry and tired people moving in and out of the house, as well as seeing to Jawana's needs.

Then the list-making began to bother me. I thought, "I have to live in this town. If I begin to say this one can come into the house and this one cannot, then I'm making distinctions among my friends that I don't want to make." So I tore the list up and told the staff just to call me to the door and let me see who would like to come in.

By this time staff, reporters, people dropping off food and supplies, and all kinds of people began to assemble at the house by the side of the road. I told Martin I needed to go to Montgomery to restock the kitchen; the local boycott was still on and Uniontown didn't offer everything I needed. I was out of just about everything: flour, cornmeal, grits, sugar, bacon, and so forth. I didn't know it, but he had put out a call for people who wanted to help the Selma movement to send food to help the households where people from out of town were staying and to the church kitchens that were feeding the marchers. A few days later, I heard a commotion in the driveway. A big truck was trying to come up the driveway but ran into the telephone lines and could not get any further. It was loaded with cases of canned string beans, hams, pork and beans, potatoes, corn, and on and on. All of the canned foods you can think of, along with household supplies. There was no way I could use all of it, even for years to come. After I stocked up, I asked that the rest be carried over to my home church, Brown Chapel African Methodist Episcopal, which was the central church for the mass meetings held in Selma.

I didn't even know myself how many people came in and out of the house by the side of the road or were living out of the church. I was truly grateful for the food and supplies and wanted to thank the many people who helped fill the truck. In my prayers I did, and maybe here I can again if this is read by someone who participated.

16
The Sanctuary

My church, Brown Chapel of the African Methodist Episcopal Church, had a close connection to the house by the side of the road, much like the relationship of our family house in York and the First Baptist Church many years before. Brown Chapel had its beginning shortly after the Civil War when Methodist missionaries from Georgia arrived to work among the freedmen. At first Selma's black Methodists met in private homes. In 1866, they came together as a group in the basement of the old Hotel Albert to decide whether to continue under white leadership or to affiliate with the African Methodist Episcopal Convention. They chose the latter. Within a year, the new congregation had been accepted as a member of the AME Convention. By 1869 a frame building was erected at the present site under the leadership of Rev. H. Stubbs. The "Brown" for whom the church is named is probably Bishop John W. Brown, though the early church records are not clear on this. John Hardy's *History of Selma* (1879) pays tribute to Brown Chapel as a splendid brick church building on Sylvan Street, capable of seating nine hundred people with regularly conducted services.

On January 2, 1965, Dr. King and Reverend Abernathy came to Selma for their first large public meeting, which was held at Tabernacle Baptist Church (my husband's church), where they both spoke and made a commitment to begin a voting rights movement in Selma. After realizing what could take place, Tabernacle pastor Rev. L. L. Anderson and the officers of the church voted to withdraw the welcome extended to Dr. King and his associates. Then a search began to find another church belonging to black people to hold the mass meetings, and large enough to accommodate the expected crowds. Contact was made with Brown Chapel. The pastor, Rev. P. H. Lewis, and officers and members called a meeting to discuss the situation. A "yes" vote came forward and an invitation was sent to Dr. King by our bishop, I. H. Bonner, who served the Ninth Episcopal District, of which our church is a part. So you see we have a lifeline of social as well as spiritual support through Brown Chapel.

Within a few days, Brown Chapel became the home of the Selma voting rights movement. The church became the heart of the movement where the foot soldiers met, ate, slept, and kept the people involved, motivated, and informed.

During these days, the house by the side of the road saw a constant flow of information and directives coming and going. Pastor Lewis was in constant contact with me and other staff at the house to make sure we knew who or what was going on at the church. Here again history has not given enough credit to Rev. P. H. Lewis, a true hero of the movement. He was on the firing line all day every day for the duration of the Selma movement. He was the shepherd of our church flock, the watchman of the facility that guided our way through the storm. I don't think people realize the huge number of persons coming in and out of the church on any given day or night. Brown Chapel was his charge along with a family of a wife and two small boys. Reverend Lewis was keenly aware of the constant danger to his family. Can you imagine the calls coming into the church office and to his home? Reporters, church members, the curious, those full of hate. Our house was in danger but the church was really on the firing line. I can imagine the fear that must have engulfed him at times, but because he was a man of God I know he talked with God, walked with God, and moved on by his faith.

With the hatred prevailing during those times, I am sure Brown Chapel was attracting attention from the violent and the deranged. Many times I asked God with his infinite mercy to watch over Reverend Lewis and his family and the church. Reverend Lewis would show me baskets of mail coming into the church, some good, some bad, some with a dollar or two to help keep the lights on and the heat going. Some of those letters contained threats I am sure he turned over to God in prayer! This was a working church: regular services were still being conducted, which meant Sunday school, communion, and other activities had to continue, as well as weddings and funerals. The work of the church never stopped. Can you imagine the pressure that must have weighed on this man?

Our hundred-year-old church took a beating for many months. After the movement left Selma and moved on to other battlefields, we were left with a worn facility that the members had to refurbish. The sacrifices we made for the good of all were paid for by a few. Even though we sent out several appeals very little money came in. If every black person who won the right to participate in our government voting would send one dollar, Brown Chapel could go down in history looking a bit better. We could have an endowment to ensure the church will always have its proper place in history and will look good inside and out. Maybe one day it will happen; I hope to see it in my lifetime.

Whenever Martin or Ralph was to speak at a mass meeting, his staff, especially those working in the community (the "street committee"), would meet beforehand at our house to discuss the event. What should be the thrust of the speech? What information should be given to the people? How should they be motivated? If the two of them were going to speak at the same event, Ralph would usually be the first speaker, warming up the crowd and could he ever. Each had his own distinct style and knew for what role he was most suited. Ralph could bring Aunt Jane right out of her seat and Martin would come and sit Aunt Jane back down into her seat with calm direction.

Many times Martin would be late getting to the church, but if the people knew he was in town, they would sit and sing until he arrived. I usually knew what the speeches would be about. Martin would sit at my little desk and write out the gist of his speech then put the papers into the trash can. Once he worked it out in his mind, he didn't need the paper. Now that I look back, why didn't I keep some of those discarded notes? What keepsakes they would have made!

1. The Jacksons' living room where meetings took place. Courtesy of the author.

2. The dining room table where meals took place at the house by the side of the road. Courtesy of Randolph Williams.

3. The bed frame of the bed where Martin Luther King Jr. slept during his visits to the house by the side of the road. Courtesy of Randolph Williams.

4. The bedside table with telephone from which King conducted business. Courtesy of Randolph Williams.

5. The desk from which King conducted business. Courtesy of Randolph Williams.

6. Sullivan and Richie Jean Jackson after their wedding. Courtesy of the author.

7. Dr. Martin Luther King Jr. and Jawana Jackson. Courtesy of the author.

8. Dr. Martin Luther King Jr. with Sullivan Jackson and daughter Jawana. Courtesy of the author.

9. Jawana and Richie Jean Jackson. Courtesy of the author.

10. Brown Chapel AME Church. Courtesy of Randolph Williams.

11. Dallas County Courthouse. Courtesy of Randolph Williams.

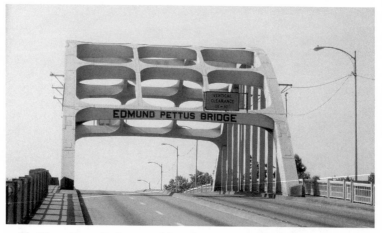

12. The Edmund Pettus Bridge, crossed during the march from Selma to Montgomery. Courtesy of Randolph Williams.

17
Vital Staff

Whenever both Dr. King and Reverend Abernathy were out of town and even sometimes when they weren't, the speaker for the mass meetings at the church would be Andrew J. Young. Either way Andy was always at the house. In the beginning we didn't know Andy as well as we knew Ralph or Martin. Here again irony comes into play. When he was a young minister from New Orleans, Andy accepted a pulpit in Marion, Alabama, and while there met and fell in love with a local young lady, Jean Childs. Her family and mine are distant cousins. I guess by now you are saying as my husband often did, "You are related to or connected with every other person in Alabama!"

After joining SCLC and having been in the organization through many campaigns, Andy came to Selma with a lot of confidence and skill. He, too, began to feel at home in the house. A gentle but strong man with deep convictions and complete loyalty to Martin Luther King Jr., he also had a special way with young people and could communicate easily with them. Martin used Andy as his second in command and trusted him with important assignments. Sometimes I sensed that Martin was disappointed with Andy and would take counsel with him in private. It wasn't Martin's way to rebuke someone publicly;

he would express himself through a joke or through a story with a particular message, but not directed at any individual.

Jawana thought the sun rose and set in Uncle Andy, that is, until he would go to sleep on the floor watching TV on her oversized stuffed dog: "Mamma, Uncle Andy is sleeping on my dog again."

"I know, but don't bother Uncle Andy, as he is tired and your dog's head just fits his. You can go into Mamma and Daddy's room, jump up in our bed, and watch TV there."

You bet she kept her eyes on her dog and Uncle Andy. The next time she caught either Andy or Hosea on her dog I was in trouble. Finally, I had to promise her I would take her shopping and she could select another dog to her liking. The notion of going shopping pleased her; after all, she was a little girl. Later when the movement had moved on, it was time that another dog be purchased to replace her poor beat up old one, so one day I took Jawana shopping. This was a terrible day for her because she could not find a stuffed dog like the one she had. Eventually we were finally able to find one that suited her and replaced the one that had been worn out by Andy and the others in the house by the side of the road.

Being a true southern gentleman from New Orleans, Andy loved good food, so at first I wondered why he was so slow to sit down at the table and eat. He would be on the phone, writing a memo, or taking notes. I finally realized that by the time he passed the stove several times, looking and tasting out of the pots, he had eaten enough to sustain himself until he finally sat down. Both he and Bernard Lee were good at that trick. I tried to prepare foods that were different from what they ate in motels or when they were away from home and couldn't get real "soul food." One of Ralph's favorites was smothered cabbage—cooked my way.

One Friday night the phone rang and I answered. "Is this the home of Dr. Sullivan Jackson?"

I replied, "Yes, who is calling?"

"A friend of his from Indiana, Jimmy Coe. I am in Selma on a hunting trip."

"Tell me where you are and I will be right there to pick you up." As I was leaving the house Sully drove up and joined me to pick up his friend. On the way back to the house, they talked about the good old times. I had no time to prepare a special meal so the men had to eat what I had already prepared that evening—salmon croquettes, smothered potatoes, cabbage, and corn muffins. Jimmy tactfully said, "Please don't put much on my plate, I am on a strict diet." We began to eat and have a wonderful conversation at dinner. All of a sudden, with a bowed head, Jimmy asked softly, "May I please have some more cabbage and another muffin?"

Sully looked up, and said, "Man, I thought you were on a diet."

"I am, but this is the best cabbage I have had since my grandmother died. Forget the diet!"

Many years later we met Jimmy Coe and his wife in Atlanta while he and Sully attended a Jazz Educators Convention. Jawana had invited all of us over to her home for dinner. The first thing Jimmy's wife said to me was, "I am so glad to see you because I am so tired of hearing about that cabbage you served Jimmy years ago and that I have been trying to fix ever since!" I was glad to be able to tell her how to fix cabbage right!

Another important member of Martin's staff was James Bevel. It was oil and water when he and Hosea were in the house by the side of the road, and I wondered what kept the roof on during their staff meetings. Boy, could they go at it. Bevel, Hosea, and James Orange were chief community organizers and in near constant motion and discussion. These were young men who strongly believed in the movement and its goals. But there were several times when Martin had to have a "come to Jesus" meeting with the staff. Sometimes Hosea, James Orange, and Bevel would, through excitement or a sense of importance, make statements to the press or give orders to the demonstrators before they had been cleared with Martin or Ralph. Martin would then counsel them; he was running a sort of leadership school for these talented young men at the same time he was leading a movement. But in the house, strong feelings or loud voices were used to convey excitement and ideas, not to show anger. The anger went in other directions.

My husband and I saw Bevel as a very strong personality with a deep commitment to the ideals of the movement and to its leader. He, too, would argue for what he felt was the right direction to pursue. But there were times when his ideas were so radical the staff needed to "pull him back in." Bevel was a brilliant and well-trained young man, and as far as the street community was concerned, he spoke their language.

There was always a shortage of sleeping space in the house but Bevel never worried about this. When he decided to sleep, he had a permanent reservation in what we call the middle bathroom. Give him a pillow and a blanket or two and the bathtub became his bed. After a while, I did not have to tell him where his bedding was; he knew and would get his own. Bevel and his wife, Diane Nash, had been with SNCC in their college days at Tennessee State and were seasoned movement veterans.

James Orange came to the staff out of the Birmingham movement. He was a very young man who had belonged to a gang in his hometown. Dr. King became aware of him and his enthusiasm and began to teach him about the strengths of the nonviolent way. James had not been a believer in nonviolence, but became a convert of Dr. King's and idealized Martin and the movement. Sometimes, however, his anger reached the point where he had to be called in for a refresher course on nonviolence that only Martin could teach. This training molded him into a totally different person. James Orange moved on as an aide to Dr. King wherever he went.

James Orange could pick James Bevel up with one arm and throw him wherever he wanted him to land. Orange was yet another big voice that would come through the back door yelling, "My leader!" Then the roof and floor would shake. James was and is a big man. He covers the ground on which he stands but he also knew what was going on in the street and at the church. He brought the news, sometimes good, sometimes bad.

One thing is certain: when they were all in the house the food would fly. For long night meetings, the kitchen was often the hub. Staff were all over the living room and dining room floors; some were asleep under the dining room table. This could go on all night. There was dinner, then late-night dinner, then sandwiches, then early breakfast (grits, bacon, eggs, and homemade biscuits), then another breakfast all over again.

Sometimes heavy hitters other than Martin or Ralph were needed. The next two people were leaders in their own right in their own communities. But they knew that Martin was the leader. They never lost their identity and Martin knew their abilities and their devotion to the movement.

When there was a special need for a speaker at the mass meetings, an envoy, a fresh voice for the many decisions that had to be made, Rev. Joseph E. Lowery was there. He was in and out of the house all of the time, even before the movement officially came to town.

Joe had been active in the movement a long time and had become a trusted friend of Martin's since the Montgomery Bus Boycott. One could say that he was a part of the "executive committee," if one existed. His thoughts, feelings, and opinions were accepted and respected. Not only did he speak in Selma, he would also go out and speak around the country instead of Ralph or Martin, and he could handle the staff when necessary. Reverend Lowery later became president of SCLC after Ralph Abernathy's death.

Reverend Lowery's wife, Evelyn Gibson Lowery, was the lady behind this man. She took a very active part when her husband became president of SCLC and she organized "SCLC Women," a group dedicated to programs for women and children. I did not know Evelyn in the early days as well as I knew the other ladies in the movement. But as the years passed a bond developed and I hope she considers me a friend.

Another firecracker, intense in every fiber of his body, was Rev. Fred Shuttlesworth of Birmingham and formerly of Selma. In the early days of his ministry he was pastor of a church just around the corner from the house by the side of the road. So we knew him, but he really took off and gained recognition during the Birmingham struggle when he was there leading another church. When he came in the house his voice, impressions, and contributions were given credence and respected. We always knew when he was in the house; his fast talking would start at the back door and not stop until he left. He would sometimes be the speaker for the mass meetings, fund-raisers, and anything else he was asked to do. Fred and Joe were always at Martin's side.

Joseph Lowery and Fred Shuttlesworth were very different in their styles of delivery. Joe was smooth and direct with a bit of humor. Fred spoke with an aggressive style, making you believe he almost hated white people. Joe would hit his point with a sparkling jab; Fred hit his with a hammer. It was a joy and an education to see them together in a staff meeting at the house. They went at it hot and heavy, especially when there were problems within the staff. Fred's short fuse seemed to be able to cut straight to the chase. For example, he would say, "Now what do you have to say, now tell me what you have to say, now this is what both of you are going to do; end of discussion."

Among all these strong personalities I thought Ralph Abernathy occasionally felt he did not get the recognition he desired. When he spoke, people really listened. I know Juanita felt that Ralph should have had more recognition of his ability inside the group and especially by the press; perhaps Martin should have had Ralph speaking for the movement more often because he could really reach the common people, where Martin was geared more toward the intellectuals. But I also remember that old saying, "There's no limit to what you can accomplish if you don't care who gets the credit." Ralph accomplished a lot.

18
Perilous Times

Sully was taking Martin to Montgomery to catch a flight during a tense period for the movement, and Sully told Martin, "Now, my gun is on the seat between us, so if a car comes up alongside that looks suspicious, you shoot while I put the pedal to the metal." Martin turned to Sully with a little laugh and said, "Sully, I thought I had taught you well and converted you to nonviolence, but it seems as if you have flunked. When we get back, I am going to have to start all over with you. You know I can't shoot anyone." Thank God they made it to Montgomery and Sully made it back without any trouble!

That evening, the staff arrived at the house for the usual meeting and told us that it was a godsend that Sully had taken Martin out the back way from the church because they had credible information that there was a sharpshooter hidden out in front, poised to kill Martin that night.

Martin began to worry about our safety in the house especially since his experience with the FBI during the Montgomery Bus Boycott taught him that he couldn't rely on them. So naturally when the Selma movement began the FBI was a factor. We knew or suspected that our phone was bugged. When or by whom we didn't know, but we felt the government would do anything it deemed necessary.

I remember after the March 7, 1965, Bloody Sunday march when a constant stream of people, both staff and reporters, were in the house and I noticed a very large Caucasian man constantly moving about in the house, and he seemed often to be where I was. Not used to this presence, I asked Martin, "Just who is this fellow? What's his connection to SCLC?" Martin smiled and quietly told me, "Jean, I think you would want to put up with him. He has been sent by the FBI to protect you." My response: "Oh!"

After that, every time I moved in and out of the house, I made sure he knew where I was. I even began to assign him tasks. "Would you mind sweeping the porch? Dr. King may want to have a news conference here." He stayed for several days and eased out just the way he had eased in. I found out later that he had been a Georgia Tech football player, which explained his solid build. I always thought the FBI knew of a specific threat to us during those days because police were everywhere. Thank God, there never was any violence against the house.

At one point, while SCLC was in town, there was a lull in the hype. There weren't as many people from the media around; sometimes there were none. A staff meeting was called at the house to see what needed to be done to bring life back to the movement. The media had to be around to take note of what was happening, otherwise the outside world would not know what was going on. The meeting was hot and heavy; idea after idea, theory after theory. Finally the decision was made for Martin and Ralph to go to jail in Selma just as they had in Birmingham. This would bring national attention back.

After much discussion, Martin and Ralph went out the next day to get arrested while leading a march from Brown Chapel to the courthouse and then back to the church. But there was no arrest, just police standing by and watching.

As we look, really look, at the city of Selma, there were two factions in the white community, the Wilson Baker group that was reasonable, intelligent, and well educated, the Jim Clark crowd, which was resistant to any change, hate-filled, and not well educated.

In the black community you had almost the same but less hate. There were those in the black community who felt things were moving too fast—they counseled, "Just give them time, white folks will come around. I am doing pretty good myself. I can get what I want, Mr. Charlie is good to me." Then there were those who had begun to ask: "Just when is Mr. Charlie going to change? He may be doing for you, but don't you want anything for your children? No, I want a better life today, now." There were divisions within each group. Then both groups would try to put up a united front. Neither side knew the conflicts within the other group. One side tried to make a new day, with equal rights and privileges for all, while the other tried to maintain the old day with the rights and privileges for a powerful few. Among the Selma whites, some counseled, "Don't arrest King and he will go away. We need to get those outside agitators out of town."

I didn't know Martin was going to the Hotel Albert, which had been an all-white establishment in downtown Selma, to register as a guest until late in the afternoon of January 18. Later, everyone returned to the house and I learned that Martin had been hit in the head. By this time you could cut the tension in the house with a knife; the events of the day had brought us to a feverish pitch. Upon returning to the house, Martin said, "Man, you can put it in the history book, that white boy can hit—but I don't know who got the worst of this confrontation. Did you see Wilson Baker pick that white fellow up by the nape of his neck and throw him into the police car? Wherever he is, he is hurting worse than I am," and fell out laughing.

Martin began to reminisce about an incident in St. Augustine, Florida, when someone hit Andy on the head and, laughing heartily, reminded Andy he was wearing an Afro at the time and it was so thick the blow never came near his scalp. Ralph, also remembering, was falling over with laughter. Andy, trying to defend himself, confessed, "It *did* hurt."

Despite their best efforts, they could not get arrested. This was one of the times when they found that humor was a good way to break the tension. Ralph and Martin would talk on the light side and have a good time with each other, resulting in great joke-telling sessions. They were really good at playing off each other when telling jokes. There was something special between those two. My husband told both of them they could have made a good living on the comedy stage. Sometimes they would have everyone in the house on the floor with laughter. Very few people saw this side of Martin and Ralph because they were usually very serious when attending to the public business of the movement. I remember one of the jokes that stands out. Martin told of an unsophisticated young country preacher who visited Atlanta for the first time. A relative took him on a tour of one of the big universities, pointing out that the grand campus buildings were named for rich benefactors who had made major gifts to the school. The preacher was impressed and decided to honor these donors as much as he could. When his children began to be born, he named his first child Dormitory, the next Cafeteria, and the third Administration. We all fell out with laughter! Martin had a gift for serious speech, but he could also tell this story in a way that made it far funnier than I have.

But the discussion always came back to serious concerns. The message in the speech for the next mass meeting had to be thought through.

Good old reliable *Webster's* dictionary describes depression as a lowering of vitality or function. There were many times I saw this condition in our beloved Martin.

Not enough sleep, not enough quiet, not enough time when there were decisions to be made, speeches to give, people to see, money to raise, problems to solve. All this in a hostile climate, where many expressed hatred and some even made threats of violence. When the body and mind find these activities too difficult to deal with, they sometimes just shut down.

When Martin found himself in a depressed state and in need of picking up, sometimes he would call Mahalia Jackson (no relation to us, unfortunately) who would counsel, console, and sing to him. Her soothing voice and quiet ministry, even over the phone, would comfort him, especially when she sang his favorite song, "Amazing Grace." In addition, when funds ran low, she would seem to be able to pull together a lot of help. What a wonderful lady. Martin really respected her and was grateful for her help. She never came to Selma but her influence was surely felt.

19
Women in the Movement

Coretta Scott King did not come to the house during this period as much as I think she may have wanted to. Maybe Martin felt one parent on the firing line was enough. The possibility of his children being without both parents may have been uppermost in his thoughts. You must remember the civil rights movement was basically run by men, and often women's input and presence did not seem needed. But how many times do women plant ideas and let the men think all of the ideas are theirs? That is the way a woman operates. We don't care who gets the credit for an idea as long as what we want gets done. Remember, I am speaking of the role of women in society half a century ago. Today's woman is very different. Coretta did come to the house by the side of the road during the turbulent days but not to stay for any period of time as was also the case with Juanita Abernathy.

I have always had a lot of respect for Coretta Scott King. Whether she was involved then really does not matter; look at what she went through—she was totally involved, right from the start, being the wife of Martin Luther King Jr. Just think: Martin's stabbing in New York. The bombing of their home in Montgomery. The many hate-filled and obscene calls she had to endure in Montgomery and Atlanta. The FBI's pernicious assaults on her husband and on their family's privacy, and throughout it all she maintained her dignity and cared for her family. Seeing her husband deeply depressed, exhausted, and physically ill had to take its toll on her. But when the time came, she took up the mantle and made a distinguished name for herself. She, too, was known all over the world for her contributions to humanity. Martin made a wise decision in picking a mate.

Even after Martin's death, Coretta used the house by the side of the road for meetings and a luncheon. Once she needed to meet attorney Fred Gray of Tuskegee, and had a meeting with him eating at the same dining room table where her husband once sat. There were other times she came to the house, especially on her way home to see her parents, Mr. and Mrs. Obie Scott in Marion, and when on speaking engagements in Selma. This house has always been open to friends, and that she was always to us.

Juanita Abernathy also came to the house during those tense and busy months, just not as much as we would have liked her to. Again, this was a man-run operation.

Juanita and Coretta were totally different in personality. Juanita was a powerful force in Ralph's life and his decision making. He would talk to her every night no matter where he was. The staff would say when Ralph and Juanita were on the phone, the president or Jesus could call and would not get through. Ralph and Juanita would be there for a while. We did not have call waiting and all of the other telephone options we have today. We had one line coming in and one line going out; if the phone was in use you just got a busy signal.

Juanita Jones came from a well-known family in Uniontown, Alabama. They owned their own land, and at that time landowners were considered "good livers." She had known Ralph and his family years before they fell in love and married. Juanita, like Ralph, had several sisters and brothers. Coming from big families, they both seemed to have the ability to deal with people from all walks of life. Juanita still has that warm glow and smile, and we have such good times when we visit. Juanita and I always had a wonderful relationship; I guess I understood some of her feelings and I always tried to be there for her and her children. I had the opportunity to attend the wedding of their youngest child, Kuami, in Atlanta. It was a special occasion for me, as all of our children are now grown and on their own. How proud we are.

Juanita was always afraid that Ralph would be hurt or killed, alone or with Martin, leaving her to raise their four children alone. She also felt Ralph was not given his proper place in history. But he was surely loved in the house by the side of the road. I had known Ralph and Juanita a lot longer than I had known Martin. We went back such a long way. When Juanita and I get together you can just hang it up because we can talk forever. Sometimes we talk all night, remembering and dreaming, not so much for ourselves anymore but for our children.

During the Selma movement, the walls of our house would be pulsating as people came and went, talking, laughing, and planning, and the telephone constantly ringing, especially if Martin was in the house. I did not know if I was coming in the front door or going out the back and answering the phone on the way. During one of Martin's visits, I expressed the need for a bit of help. Realizing what I needed, he asked Dora McDonald to come and help and she did, arriving not a moment too soon. The momentum was building for the big march to Montgomery. If help was ever needed, it was needed then—just answering the telephone was a full-time job.

Dora was Martin's secretary at SCLC in Atlanta. She really knew all the ins and outs, who the people were, what to say, and how to keep up with all the paperwork, records, and so on. She was a calm and effective person who never seemed to get excited or distracted by anything or anybody.

20
Other Support Systems

How did we ever do without the telephone? When God gave Alexander Graham Bell the inspiration and knowledge to invent the telephone, he surely knew what people needed, although with one advancement we lost the benefits of another. Before the telephone, we wrote more, all the beautifully written letters and documents that history has preserved for us. The thoughts that went into conveying what we wanted to say to each other were once exclusively on paper. We no longer write letters, now we just pick up a phone!

If we had recorded what the phones in this house had heard, what a story that would tell of conversations carried on, decisions made that would affect our lives, and the history that was made. It would be interesting to know who was listening in or recording our calls— in today's language, "Big Brother." I still have the telephones Dr. King used to talk with President Johnson late at night.

During the early days of the movement, the South Central Bell Telephone Company called the house to speak to Dr. Sullivan Jackson. I responded, "This is Mrs. Jackson. Dr. Jackson is not here, may I take a message?"

"We noticed your phone bill has jumped up drastically from the normal monthly amount and we wondered if there is a problem." I smiled and assured them that we were indeed aware of the increase in usage and the bill would be paid in full, on time as usual. Thanking them for their concern, I hung up. I guess they would wonder why the bill had jumped from twenty dollars a month to over eight hundred!

There were people I never saw but voices I came to know well such as Rev. Thomas Kilgore of California, a trusted advisor of Martin's. I was never able to put a face with his voice because he did not come to the house. Then there were Bayard Rustin and attorney Jack Greenburg, both of whom called regularly from New York. When I heard these two voices I knew to get Martin or someone from the staff on the phone. These calls were always accepted. Their voices were easily identified because they called so often. Jack Greenburg would call frequently during the planning sessions; he did come to the house once, but Bayard Rustin never came, which a disappointment for me because I wanted to meet this famous civil rights leader and put a face with this quiet, cultured voice.

There were also calls I learned to defer or put off and may God forgive me but when I knew Martin needed some rest I would say, "I am sorry he is unavailable at this time." Reporters from all over the world would call wanting another interview or just to be in Martin's presence over a telephone. There were calls expressing bitterness, threats, and just plain hate, but you do what you have to do and move on to the next call. You feel sorry for those who let hate and ignorance take up so much space in their hearts. I wonder, is there room in their hearts for love? Do we as human beings understand God's mandate to love one another as he loves us? How can we as Christians serve the same God, read his word, worship in his houses, and yet let hate fester in our hearts?

There were others calling that I knew needed to get through, especially Randolph Blackwell, because he was on SCLC's staff and an advising attorney. He was also the liaison between other organizations cooperating with SCLC and the movement. Rev. Wyatt T. Walker, who had been a longtime civil rights leader, spokesman, and activist in his own right, as well as a friend and confidant of Dr. King's, was allowed to speak to Martin. He had been onboard since Dr. King's early days in Montgomery and was even selected to be one of the first executive directors of SCLC. From 1955 onward he accepted important assignments and gave sound advice. Even from the Selma jail Martin sent him requests.

Some called and then came by in person. Some meetings were held to make different organizations and leaders feel a part of the movement. One such person who came to the house was John Lewis of SNCC (Student National Coordinating Conference). He was very much involved in the Selma movement and later became a U.S. congressman from Georgia. Another SNCC leader, Bernard Lafayette, was active in Selma. SNCC was working on voter registration in and around rural communities in Selma and Dallas County long before SCLC came in. This did cause some friction between the two organizations. SNCC had been working for several years with very little publicity or funds. SCLC came in and overnight the press arrived and money began to come in as well. Money and a place in the sun can bring egos to a boiling point, and they did.

SNCC and James Farmer, their executive secretary and spokesman, felt if there were to be a Selma movement, SNCC should share some of the spotlight and funding. Discussions about who should be in a photo-op, who should lead the march, methodology, and future benefits were held in the house. Sometimes the sessions would get hot and heavy. Sometimes the participants came away satisfied, and many times discussions had to be continued. Not only did this organization have some very strong feelings, but also the local group, the Dallas County Voters League, began to come in with the same petition—they wanted their share of the limelight and money. What these other groups didn't fully understand was the money they thought was coming in was going out just as fast, and that to get those precious few dollars one man was working night and day—Martin Luther King Jr.

Martin would listen to everybody and make them all feel important. He would hear and accept their concerns and feel their pain, and whether they came away with anything or not, at least they felt better for having been listened to. I saw this occur many times.

Another visitor, but one I never felt I really knew, was James Foreman of SNCC, although he was in the house several times and provided the movement with sound strategy. His face and eyes portrayed only business—no chitchat. He was an intense person, and when he was not in a meeting he had little to say, but would sit quietly and thoughtfully, eating fresh oranges. I would find orange rinds everywhere in the house—in flower pots, on a shelf, anywhere he could find to stick them. I still have a pipe he left behind on one of his trips. Overalls were his preferred attire, and he wore them all of the time, only asking for a washcloth and towel. I never saw him in anything but overalls and often wondered how many pairs he must have had! Foreman was a brilliant man with very strong ideas and convictions and plans who wanted to see his organization grow and realize its potential. SNCC and SCLC had the same goals but different paths to reach those goals.

Representative John Conyers from Michigan came to show his support as well as give advice from a national government view point. I don't remember how he arrived, but my husband and I took him to Birmingham to catch a flight back to Washington. During his visit and the trip to the airport we had a chance to talk with him and let him know what we thought the needs of the movement were and what progress we felt was being gained. He vowed to do anything he could, and he remained one of our strongest leaders in Congress.

Another strong supporter who came to the house was Martin's brother, Rev. A. D. King. We had known A. D. for several years, although not as well as Martin. He had been in the house before the Selma movement got under way while attending one of the Baptist state meetings at Selma University, when our friends in that group would all show up at the back door.

One especially interesting meeting was held in our daughter's room; Martin, in his pajamas, was half-sitting, half-lying, on Jawana's bed. On the right side of the bed was Ralph in his pajamas. Andy Young was sitting on the floor. Bernard Lee, C. T. Vivian, and James Bevel were all crowded into the room. Hosea was sitting at the foot of the bed on Ralph's side. A. D. then came in and greeted his brother and the others and sat at the foot of the bed on Martin's side. Serious discussions and strategizing were under way.

I was somewhere in the house, probably in the kitchen cooking, when all of a sudden I heard a loud crash. I stopped in my tracks to make up my mind where the sound originated from, then flew to the bedroom to find everyone in an uproar. The bed had collapsed to the floor! Everyone was doubled over with laughter. All I could see were feet. Martin turned to Ralph and said, "I told you, you need to lose some weight. Now you have smashed the bed!" Ralph was smiling and telling A. D. he was the last to sit on the bed, so he broke it. Hosea was standing straight up and yelling, "My leader, it wasn't me!" I walked in and put them all out to assess what damage had been done. They all moved into the living room, just beyond the door of the bedroom. Martin, bringing the group back to some kind of order, continued the discussion.

The rail on Ralph's side of the bed was split in half. Now you must realize that was some weight for any bed. Ralph was over 200 pounds, Hosea also over 200, Martin came in about 175, and A. D. was well over 250! Knowing I could not do without a bed, I called a friend of ours—a fellow church member, Robert Perry—to come quickly to fix the break or do whatever he could to put the bed back into service. This was done, and the bed patched up for use until more permanent repairs could be made. Jawana still uses the bed whenever she comes home to the house by the side of the road. She has often remarked over the years that whenever she is in this bed she feels protected from all of life's harm!

When comedian and activist Dick Gregory entered the house you started laughing even before he opened his mouth. A staunch supporter of everything that dealt with civil rights, he always had a joke to tell, but if you listened closely to what everyone thought was funny, there was also a real message of truth from a heart that was all serious. He was and to this day is willing to do all he can to make this country treat all of its citizens with dignity and justice. He also could put everyone at ease and discharge any tension in a serious situation. This meant a lot to all of us and made his coming that much more enjoyable. I wish I could remember some of the jokes and conversations we had, but they wouldn't sound the same without his skill in telling them.

Just the opposite feelings occurred when James Baldwin, the famed black writer, came to see Dr. King and bring "a piece of change" to the movement. The atmosphere then was very different. He was entirely serious and, reading some of his writing later, I could see he had a brilliant mind.

Everyone had a personal strength to contribute, which made each person a special part of the movement.

21

Nobel Prize Winners
in the House

During the preparations for the march to Montgomery, among the demonstrations and all the activity, we did experience a quiet moment in the house by the side of the road. Martin asked Dr. Ralph Bunche, winner of the Nobel Peace Prize, to come to Selma. If I did not know the history and had not the benefit of my own experiences, I wonder if I would believe how fate and life could really connect. Remember my mother, always seeking better opportunities for me, had sent me to live in Washington, D.C., with my Uncle Harold. There I would finish Banneker Junior High School and Cardoza High School. This will all make sense in just a little while.

I received a call one afternoon, and the woman on the other end of the line asked, "Is this the home of Dr. Sullivan Jackson?"

I replied, "Yes, it is."

"Is this Richie Jean Sherrod Jackson?"

I now began to wonder what this was all about. The lady continued: "This is Jane Bunche. Do you remember me? We were classmates at Banneker Junior High School. I know it has been a long time!"

"Jane!" I replied. "Yes, I remember you! How many times did I come in and out of your house on the Howard University campus? How are you?"

"Fine," she replied. We went on and on for awhile, catching up on all that had happened over the years. Then she told me her father, Dr. Ralph Bunche, was determined to come to Selma to meet with Dr. King. Because of his health problems, she really did not want her father to travel, but since Dr. King had invited him to my home and she knew me, she hoped I would take special care of him.

I was delighted to renew an old friendship and even more delighted to have her father in our home—a man whom I had long admired. I dusted the house especially well for this visitor and was overjoyed to have an occasion to see Dr. Bunche again after so many years and in my own home. I immediately began to press the sheets he was to sleep on with great care. I had not ironed a sheet in months with the turnover I was experiencing, but this guest was different and special.

Martin was at the house to greet Dr. Bunche when he arrived and I just had to have a word with him. He and I visited, and I brought him up to date on my life since he had last seen me and proudly introduced him to Jawana. Dr. Bunche and Martin began to discuss their concerns. Although Dr. Bunche was getting up in age and was diabetic along with other frailties, he was determined to speak at the mass meeting that evening at the church. I retired to my usual place in the kitchen to prepare a special meal for them both. The meal consisted of what I thought would be two meals because Jane had carefully informed me of her father's strict diet.

Martin never liked a heavy meal before a mass meeting. He preferred to eat after the gathering. This time, however, he came into the kitchen and told me he would eat whatever I was preparing for Dr. Bunche. He also knew of his special diet. I prepared broiled chicken, cottage cheese, egg salad, canned peaches (no sugar), crackers, and hot tea. Dr. Bunche came into the kitchen, and then moved on into the dining room where Dr. King was already seated. At that moment, a wonderful realization came into my mind, one that brought a powerful feeling over me like a warm spring wind after a cold winter. I had two Nobel Peace Prize winners sitting at my dining room table! How remarkable that was. Dr. Bunche was a quiet and gentle man, and his presence seemed to make the house peaceful. For some reason, the house that day was not fully occupied by the usual staff members. This calmer atmosphere allowed the two men to spend some quality time together, planning and hoping to solve the world's problems.

I felt so wonderful, I wanted to tell someone what was happening in our home. I woke my husband up. As usual my husband took a nap after supper no matter what was happening or who was in the house. He would greet guests, offer to get them anything they needed, then disappear to our bedroom. Just before exiting, he would make the standard announcement to all: "My wife will see to it that your stay is pleasant."

After waking my husband, I told him that Dr. Bunche was in the house, sitting at our dining room table with Martin, and I told him of my excitement at having two such guests. He pulled me close to him, kissed me, and said, "I am glad you are getting some joy for all of your work. I will speak to him later." With that, he turned over and went back to sleep!

After that evening's mass meeting several staff members came back to the house as usual. They also had the utmost respect for this gentle soldier who had been on the battlefield for human rights for such a long time all over the world. Naturally, there was the usual discussion regarding how well the meeting went, an analysis of the different speeches or statements, what was the pulse of the crowd jam-packed into the church, the remarks from the audience, and what brought applause from the people. The staff was eager to let Dr. Bunche know how well he had been received and the respect the audience had for him.

Later in another session at the house, Dr. Bunche sat holding court, giving advice and telling all to stay the course. As an educator at Howard University, a longtime statesman, an undersecretary at the United Nations, a Nobel Peace Prize recipient, a diplomat, and a negotiator, he could bring much experience and skill to the movement and would be received with credibility and respect. Martin knew all of this and appreciated his being in Selma, and listened intently. Dr. Bunche seemed to come alive while advising us on strategy for this latest battle for freedom.

Jane called to check in on her father and to see how well the speech at the evening's meeting had gone. Pleased to know how well he felt and had done, she gave her permission for him to symbolically participate in the coming second march to Montgomery. Naturally he could not go the fifty-mile distance, so he went over the Edmund Pettus Bridge to begin the march but then was driven to Montgomery for the last events of the day. Here again, this honored man that the world had taken special note of still had the will to march for human freedom. It was brilliant strategy by King and his team, but it was also deeply meaningful for those who gathered to change history.

22

Soldiers in the Storm

Another soldier in the movement was a young minister named Nelson Smith. I say soldier because his first major battles were fought in the streets of Birmingham, Alabama.

He began the battle with his fellow clergy Fred Shuttlesworth, A. D. King, John Porter, and John H. Cross, the pastor of Sixteenth Street Baptist Church, the church where four little girls were horribly killed by a bomb in September 1963. These four little girls, dressed in their Sunday best, attending Sunday school class, in their church worshiping God, were no threat to anyone and had no hate for anyone. Why?

These men were the pillars of the fight—but the struggle did not end in Birmingham. There were issues and rights that still had to be pursued. We had in no way reached the Promised Land nor had we gained the right to be full citizens with the right to vote in the country of our birth. Birmingham had successfully desegregated hotels, motels, and drinking fountains, but we still had a long way to go and much to do.

Many soldiers, generals, lieutenants, and foot soldiers came through the house by the side of the road, all in the service of the movement.

Some we knew, others we did not. Some were old friends and many became lifelong friends as a result of this great cause.

Reverend Smith was in and out of the house to support, assist, speak, or do whatever was needed for the Selma movement. He would drive Martin Luther King Jr. to Selma if he came by air to Birmingham.

We will never know just how many people were out to kill Martin Luther King Jr., but Nelson told us about one case in which he was involved. He was about to bring Martin to Selma one night, but word reached them of a plot against their lives. So instead of driving Nelson's car they switched to a U.S. marshal's car. The perpetrators were thrown off by the car change. If the switch had not been made, both might have been killed that night. The car was filled with tension, and watchful eyes moved all around as they traveled to Selma on those dark, winding back roads.

Rev. Nelson Smith never forgot us or the role we played in the Selma movement. Over the years, he invited us to his church to be honored. Not only does he remember but he would come to the house by the side of the road several times a year, just as the old group did when going to Selma University for the Baptist meetings, and without fail he would come to say hello or to sit for a while and just reminisce. We would sit at the same dining room table and have a meal together once again.

Another SNCC soldier working in the community was a very strong young man named John Lewis, who today is a U.S. congressman from Georgia. Lewis represented the strength in young people and their convictions regarding human rights for all. Today, I consider him the "conscience of our Congress" as he strives to carry on Dr. King's principles each day through the halls of America's government. John Lewis continues to fight the good fight. He has made his own indelible mark on the battlefields for civil rights, and continues to challenge us all in the work for peace and justice. Bloodied but unbowed, John Lewis is still trying to make America a great country for all.

On the day of the Bloody Sunday march over the bridge in Selma, March 7, 1965, John Lewis and Hosea Williams headed the line and were attacked, injured, and scarred. Lewis was beaten over the head and kicked about his body, resulting in a fractured skull and many bruised ribs. But God was on his side for he still had work for him to do.

John Lewis was in and out of the house on a regular basis, in strategy sessions, and was very much a part of all that was going on. He was SNCC staff but worked closely with SCLC in those critical days. I never knew if he actually switched organizations or not, but I do know he gave his all and was a very trusted ally. John had an open door to Dr. King, who valued his youthful strength and grasp of the issues. If there were ever conflicts between SNCC and SCLC over who was getting funds or had the most attention from the media, John Lewis was always above the fray.

Joseph T. Smitherman was the young mayor of Selma when the civil rights movement came to town. My husband and I knew him prior to his becoming mayor because he was a partner with his brother-in-law in an appliance company, and after we were married, we purchased several appliances from their store. Mr. Smitherman had been in and out of the house by the side of the road on several occasions to deliver an appliance or to perform maintenance, so he was no stranger to us. He treated us well and was friendly because we were putting bread in his mouth. Perhaps we weren't seeing his true feelings. Perhaps since Smitherman was not a polished, experienced politician and was a very young man at the time, he had to follow the lead of city fathers who had put him in power, whether his heart told him differently or not.

One must understand the climate of the white south—to relinquish power and control was just unthinkable. The idea of more black voters brought forth untold fear. Yes, there were a few black voters in the community, but not enough to make any difference in the power structure, and many of those registered were told who and who not to vote for.

Can you imagine the pressure Smitherman was under with Gov. George Wallace telling him what to do? The white power structure in the city was also giving him instructions. Col. Al Lingo of the Alabama State Patrol came to Selma and Dallas County, placed his troops at the edge of the city, and told Smitherman how to handle the masses of black protestors, warning the young mayor that he must prevent blacks from "taking over the city." He also had to contend with Sheriff Jim Clark, who was employed by Dallas County and not answerable to the mayor. Bless his heart, he was having a hard time! Can you imagine Dr. Martin Luther King Jr., a Nobel Peace Prize winner, sitting in his jail along with Ralph Abernathy, another black firebrand who was from nearby Marengo County, all this and hundreds of blacks from his own city, protesting constantly against injustice, with all of the rest of the country and even the world seeing Selma on television and in the newspapers everyday?

As time marched on and more and more blacks registered to vote, Smitherman learned the political game and saw he needed that vote to continue in power. Therefore, as all politicians do, he learned to play the game to get the votes necessary to stay in office. Through the years he learned the game well. He went where he needed to go and said to each group what needed to be said to make them happy and garner the vote. Black voters, having such a forgiving soul, kept him in office longer than any other mayor Selma ever had.

23
Preparing for the March

There were marches and there were marches, but I do not know if anyone can give an exact number of people who participated, not only in Selma but in many of the small rural towns throughout the Black Belt. Dr. King did not lead all of the marches, and was in Atlanta during the famed Bloody Sunday march.

The idea of a march from Selma to Montgomery, the capital of Alabama, came about the night Jimmy Lee Jackson was shot in Marion, February 18, 1965. There had been so much discussion about the march, including whether it should take place at all, especially since there were rumors flying around as to whether Gov. George Wallace and Sheriff Jim Clark and his posse of volunteer white segregationists would permit such a march without some causing serious problems. In addition, Dr. King and those around him were receiving death threats. Along Highway 80, the route the march was planned to take, were stands of trees, swamps, and other areas that would give cover to snipers, especially in Lowndes County, which had an even worse reputation than Dallas County for violence and far fewer registered black voters.

The decision was finally made to go forward with a march set for

March 7, 1965. Hosea in particular felt that the time was right and the people were ready. Dr. King was in Atlanta but was expected to lead the march on Monday, March 8, or Tuesday the ninth, not Sunday as planned. Hosea and James called Ralph Abernathy that Sunday morning telling him it was time to go and that it would be too dangerous for Dr. King because of the many threats. So they decided that Dr. King should stay in Atlanta and preach that Sunday.

As I told you earlier Hosea would be given a directive, and if that directive did not suit his thinking he would set about doing things his way as he convinced Dr. King and Reverend Abernathy at the last minute to let him and John Lewis go on the front line. Getting John Lewis to go with him also went a long way toward including SNCC, which would also help the two groups bond.

We found out there were meetings taking place all over town. Fear began to run rampant, especially in the white community. Word had reached them of the pending march. There was also fear in the black community. The same question was asked in both communities: "What will happen if the march is held?" I always wondered how the white community found out about the march since the decision was only made the morning of the march. How did they find out so quickly? Was the church phone or our home phone bugged?

I was not at the church the Sunday of the first march. With the house empty, I took the opportunity to catch up on some household chores such as changing linen, washing towels, and so forth. It was a good thing we had a washer and dryer! Sully and I had received an abundance of sheets and towels when we married so I had no shortage of linen. I was well stocked.

While doing the things that needed to be done, a thought came over me: "Remember the Sabbath day and keep it holy." I stopped and prayed, "Lord, forgive me for my sin of labor on the Sabbath, but you know I have to get this done for they all will be back tomorrow." I have always tried to keep this commandment in the many years that have followed. Later during the day I asked for forgiveness again for fear he did not hear me the first time!

24
Strategy

What the law enforcement officers and state troopers did not know was that the staff had not planned to go all the way to Montgomery that day, only over the bridge, then stop to kneel and pray, and then return to Brown Chapel. But once upon the bridge, they saw the confrontation that would happen. There were state troopers under Al Lingo, Sheriff Jim Clark and his mounted vigilantes, and hordes of onlookers jeering with all kinds of ugly language. Can you imagine what fear must have engulfed the marchers, thinking they were surely facing injury and death? Just think of the courage and dedication it took to keep on walking over the span of that bridge, not knowing what would happen next.

Word had spread in the white community that the march would indeed take place. Churches must have let the congregations out early for so many people to be there and ready. I guess they could not stand to see a peaceful group of Negroes walking through "their streets" and over "their bridge" just asking for the right to cast a ballot to decide who should govern them and the laws under which they should live. The marchers had tear gas thrown at them, and law officials on horseback with electric cattle prods set to kicking and beating, knocking down and trampling people with the hooves of horses, and turning on the fire hoses and hitting the marchers randomly. Blood was flowing, people were down, eyes damaged because of the gas, limbs broken, heads smashed, yet somehow all managed to get back to Brown Chapel.

The marchers did not use the route they had taken to reach the bridge to get back to the church; they used any street that would get them back safely. Thank God for the media that day, for they saw, recorded, and taped the events and immediately sent the reports to their broadcast outlets so that it could be seen on the Sunday evening news by the entire world.

My husband and other black doctors in Selma spent the afternoon patching up the injured. My uncle, Fred Williams, who owned a funeral home, provided his hearses for use as ambulances to pick up the tear-gassed and beaten marchers along the route of the march. Sully, my cousin Dr. William B. Dinkins, and Dr. Eddie Maddox were in the back of the hearses prepared with emergency medical supplies for all who needed it. One person who needed care on that afternoon was Mrs. Marie Foster, my husband's sister. After arriving at Good Samaritan Hospital (the only facility in town that would treat the injured black marchers) with some of the injured, Sully found Marie on a gurney in the hospital hallway bleeding from the head. He quickly saw to her wounds and found out that she and Mrs. Amelia Boynton had been in the third or fourth row in the line of marchers. Both Marie and Mrs. Boynton were part of a local civil rights group known as the "Courageous Eight."

Word passed through the city very quickly. Every telephone in the city jumped off the hook. Did you see the evening news? Do you believe what you saw? How can white people hate so much? I was surprised to learn nobody had been killed. No matter where you were or what you may have been doing, all able bodies headed to Brown Chapel.

I had seen a lot of people at my church previously, but that night I truly believe 80 percent of all black people in Selma and the surrounding area showed up at the church. And the other 20 percent came to the house by the side of the road!

When I returned home I do believe reporters must have come up from the ground like mushrooms, given the short amount of time it took them to reach the house. Dr. King was still in Atlanta but was quickly made aware of what was happening in Selma. I told reporters that Dr. King was not here over and over again. Didn't they realize if he had been in Selma he would have been at the church or at the hospital? I felt they thought I was hiding him. By now I was getting angry, maybe not so much with the reporters but I was very upset over the events of the day. My emotions started to get raw, confused, and rush through my system. The doorbell rang constantly and the telephone was ringing off the hook. I even considered putting the phone in the toilet, but with my luck it would continue to ring even in there! I am glad I didn't, because a conference call started between the staff at the house and many others around the country. What are the ramifications of today's actions? Who will deal with the press? Has the president called? And, by the way, make a list of all who do call over the next twenty-four hours!

25
The Fires Burn

Martin and Ralph arrived in Selma early the next morning on Monday, March 8, 1965. Staff was in and out all that day, meeting, making phone calls, and seeking a court injunction in Montgomery to permit another march, and evaluating the information that came in from national news and from overseas as to what the rest of the world had seen. How were the people who were sent to the hospital? Dr. King decided he needed to go see them sometime during the day, especially before the mass meeting started that evening.

After learning about the events of the previous afternoon and before he left Atlanta Dr. King made a call for clergy from all over the country to come to Selma to take a stand against violence, and come they did. A young white Unitarian minister named James Reeb arrived from Boston and marched in Selma on Tuesday, March 9, with Dr. King. Later that evening after getting some dinner at a downtown restaurant, Reverend Reeb and several other ministers were returning to the church and passed a hangout for whites, where four white men jumped Reeb's party and began beating him with a baseball bat. Reverend Reeb lapsed into a coma and was taken to Birmingham to the University Hospital; it was feared that Reverend Reeb could not get the quality medical care he needed in Selma. After all, he was viewed as an outside agitator and, even worse, an outside white agitator siding with blacks. Can you imagine how all of this made us feel? This young man leaving the comforts of his home and his family to join us in our struggle had been attacked brutally. Reverend Reeb died from his injuries a few days later and we all prayed for his soul. The whole country was in indignation over his death, but sad to say where was the same outcry when Jimmy Lee Jackson was mortally wounded in Marion fighting for the very same things? The difference was clear: Jimmy Lee Jackson was a black man; Rev. James Reeb was white.

As the Reverend Anderson set out on a ministers' march on March 10, Mayor Smitherman and public safety director Wilson Baker put a rope, a noose, around the area of the church. He said no marchers could leave the area immediately surrounding the church. He set up police barriers all around. You could go into the mass meetings at the church but getting out sometimes became a problem. We were at the church that night with my mother and other members of our family. I knew I needed to leave the church and return home; but how would I get there? As I stated earlier, my family owned J. H. Williams and Sons Funeral Home, which is now over a hundred years old. Someone in the family suggested that we call and have an ambulance from the funeral home to come to the church.

We told the police that someone had become ill and needed to be taken to the hospital. When the vehicle arrived, my family members and I piled in, turned the lights and siren on, and rushed right past the police. As you know, where there is a will there is a way. We as a people are very resourceful in finding a way out of no way!

Dr. King was in the house often during this period going to and from Montgomery, applying in court to get an injunction allowing us to march to Montgomery. He was also putting out fires that erupted almost daily from everywhere including SNCC. Here in the house by the side of the road we felt that the movement had gained momentum and was still growing. SNCC was threatening to pull out and to a point they did. If Dr. King was pushed aside because of absence or illness, SNCC would move to take over the spotlight. But who was bringing in the outside support and making effective calls for ministers to come? Who was rallying the nation behind us? Who brought in enough money to supply the movement's needs as well as giving SNCC financial assistance? Looking at the bigger picture, John Lewis stayed on King's team. I guess he felt that since he had suffered a concussion crossing the bridge for the movement and walked a long way from his hometown of Troy, Alabama, he had come too far to give up. He was committed.

I can remember one session with James Foreman, here in the house when not only the tension was high but the language was rough and voices loud. Sometimes your major fears and worries can come from within. But when James Orange and Hosea Williams were in the house you came to realize much of the rhetoric and threats were just that. Their voices were raised with passion because of what they were doing and out of true devotion to their leader, Martin.

Dr. King also realized that too much hasty or combative rhetoric outside the house could become a real problem and create a sense that was not all was calm and steady in the leadership. There would be problems and conflicting opinions; most I heard or knew about, and most were eventually resolved behind closed doors here at the house by the side of the road. I didn't care to witness those sessions. No matter what the emotions or disagreements were, we should always leave the house united.

Dr. King had pulled together a moving memorial service on the steps of the Perry County Courthouse in Marion for Jimmy Lee Jackson on March 3. He said then that was one of the most difficult eulogies he had ever delivered. Now Jimmy Lee was being joined by other casualties in the battle for freedom, and Dr. King came to Selma for a service for James Reeb on March 15.

On returning to the house after the service, Dr. King was in constant contact with the White House, telling the president and his aides that he really needed to make a statement to the country about the situation. They talked about some points the president needed to make. Finally, President Johnson made the decision to speak to the nation. What we would later hear from the president would help change history.

Late that afternoon we had dinner and settled in to watch and listen to the president's speech to Congress that night. Several staff members were at the house, including Andy Young and Bernard Lee, and this was the first time Rev. Jesse Jackson was in the house. My mother had also come by to watch the speech with us—in other words, every chair was taken and even the floor was full! We were all in the living room in front of the television. I was sitting on the floor at Martin's feet. The speech began and all were quiet until a "Wow!" here or a "Well!" was cried out during the speech. As the president got near the end of his speech and spoke the words "We shall overcome," the whole house fell silent in disbelief. I turned and looked up at Martin and saw a tear sliding down his check. The moment was almost too much for him to handle. What could you say to this man at such a moment? Did I really hear what I thought I heard the president say? Is Martin really crying?

I had never looked at or thought of a piece of furniture as being anything but useful. Some pieces are beautiful for their lines and craftsmanship, but there is one chair in our house that we have developed a special love for. The chair that Martin sat in that night remains just as it did then. A photographer from *Life* magazine was in the house that night and took a photo that later was featured in the magazine article on the Selma movement and showed Dr. King sitting in that chair watching the president's address on that historic night. It sits there still, nearly a half century later, and I take particular pride in pointing out that silent witness to history.

After the president's speech, there was another almost all-night session with phone calls coming in from everywhere. Dr. King spoke to President Johnson after the speech that night. Reporters were calling for responses and coming to the house to get a reaction. Thank God for Bernard Lee that night.

Sprits were very low the next day. The excitement of the night before had given way a sense of the realities of the task before us. Martin spent a lot of time at the church. He would come back to the house by the side of the road to get a bath and to eat a good meal when I insisted that he eat something. After the emotional high point of the president's expression of support for voting rights, depression really began to set in. But when you are busy and there are so many pulling on you for this and that with decisions that have to be made you somehow go on as best you can, and Martin did.

James Reeb's death and the country's shock and disbelief at the events in Selma had really put pressure on President Johnson to give some thought to meaningful civil rights legislation. The president had promised much in his speech, but was it all just lip service or would it be followed by action?

When the country began to really wake up and the pressure began to reach Washington, D.C., the president knew he had to go beyond the promises he was giving Martin Luther King Jr. that the government would bar the literacy test for voting and end the poll tax. The president had seemed to be saying, "We will get around to doing something, so stop pushing." But more was needed and demanded. Several times the phone rang late at night and the voice on the other end used a code to let us know the president was calling for Martin. During one of those late-night phone calls, Martin told the president about conditions in Selma and in the movement, and called for a complete restructuring of the voting rights legislation. This made the president angry, but Martin thought he had nothing to lose with the tide of support from the country on his side.

After these conversations, Martin realized he needed to be ready to ask the president for specific things, so he told Andy to get the staff he needed to pull together a draft of a strong voting rights bill. That bill was drafted right here in the house by the side of the road around the dining room table with many saying the language was not strong enough, and others arguing the need to create a bill that Congress would pass. Everyone had recommendations and warnings, so the discussions went on and on.

Telephone calls were made to lawyers around the country about legal language. The staff called congressmen and other government leaders to see what language would likely be accepted and still get the job done.

After the bill was written, dissected, rejected, and finally approved, Martin put the finishing touches on the document. Then he felt he had a bill he could bring before the president. Johnson would know just what to tell the Justice Department to draft before he took the bill to Congress. If you don't ask or spell out what you want, you may never get it. We wanted "one man, one vote" and nothing less.

At last the injunction that Dr. King and our lawyers had sought in federal courts in Montgomery and Mobile that would prevent Alabama officials from stopping a march had come through. Then the president nationalized the Alabama National Guard to protect the marchers. The second march would go forward, not just over the bridge but all the way to Montgomery, the state capital and the home of Gov. George Wallace.

26
On Our Way

Now the flurry of action begins. Locate campsites, because the trip cannot be made in one day. Find the black-owned land along the road between Selma and Montgomery, where marchers can rest and eat along the way. Secure portable toilets; set up transportation for the supplies the marchers would need: water, food.

We had to check weather forecasts carefully, as they would be vital to the success of the march; we did not have the Weather Channel available then. Should SNCC be counted in the numbers of march supporters? How long will the march take? Who will walk all the way to Montgomery and who will ride? These were some of the issues that had to be figured out.

We really need people now! If we ever needed bodies at all, now is the time! We need persons from all walks of life, all races, all creeds, all professions, high- and low-profile people. We need people to leave with us from Selma, then more to join in Montgomery. The press has to be notified immediately. We need a firm commitment from at least two of the major television stations out of Montgomery that they will send a crew to accompany the march all the way—every step of this march must be documented. We also needed money to fund such a huge campaign; where would it come from?

Assignments were divided up among staff and off they went. Calls were pouring in from everywhere. Correct information had to be given to reporters; staff were coming in with new information, then there were additional problems popping up to be dealt with. Every one was busy. I did not know if I was coming or going, probably doing both. At the same time beds had to be changed, food had to be prepared, bathrooms cleaned, towels washed and folded. And on it went. We had less than a week to prepare—we were to march on Sunday, March 21. Thank God for Dora McDonald and Bernard Lee. I could not have made it without them. While the plans were being made security was the top priority, so I could not bring anyone from the outside into the house to help me in my work. We all just had to pitch in and get it done the best way we could.

Andy was told to get on the phone and report to the major supporters and organizations on the injunction that allowed the march, and the nationalization of the Alabama National Guard and the dispatch of federal marshals to protect the marchers. This would help reduce some of the fears outsiders might have about coming to Alabama. Somewhere along the way in the midst of all the planning, a thought came to my mind. Are these calls and this information going out to the right people? Will the wrong ears also hear? The wrong ears could then try to stop the march before it starts. I really felt uneasy about Brown Chapel and about whether this historic place to worship would be a target or if Martin Luther King Jr. would be in danger as head of the movement. When there is evil in a man's heart there is no telling what that man may do. How do people protect themselves from evildoers?

Dr. King, Reverend Abernathy, and SCLC staff were in and out of the house. Quickly, church after church, organization after organization was notified and came onboard for the second march. People began to plan to come by plane, train, bus, car, and foot. Word reached one of this country's most eminent black scholars and historians, Dr. John Hope Franklin. Nothing took place in this country regarding black Americans without Dr. Franklin's input. Knowing the struggle so well, he came to Selma and convinced a large group of fellow historians from all over the country to join him.

Peter Hall and Orzell Billingsley, attorneys from Birmingham, Alabama, who had been in the house on many previous occasions, put out the call for lawyers to join us as a "must do in support of the movement," and attorneys from all over the country heeded the call and converged on Selma. Black, white, brown, and yellow Americans from all over this land descended on our small city in the hope of fulfilling a dream that would benefit everyone.

27
No Room in the Inn

Everything was moving into place. People were traveling to Selma in faith that all would be well, as days and nights passed until we realized it was the night before the day of the big march.

That night reporters began to come in and camp out. They were all over the place. The church was packed and twice as many were sitting and standing on the outside. The housing project that stands around the church was filled to capacity. Residents of the projects allowed thousands of visitors here for the march to stay in their already cramped and crowded apartments. Everyone was supportive. The house by the side of the road was overflowing. There were many dignitaries in my home, some of whom I knew and many I did not. Sully and I just tried to be gracious hosts given the sheer number of people and the circumstances that had brought us all together. There were doctors, lawyers, ministers, and heads of organizations, powerful people from all over the country at the house.

Dr. King and Reverend Abernathy, who were always side by side, were both exhausted. Ralph, with his calm attitude, said, "We have done all we can." Ralph and Martin then went into the bedroom to pray that all would go well and ask God to take care of everyone for everything was in his hands now.

Martin, totally exhausted and coming down with another cold, finally went to bed. A physician from New York sat in the doorway outside his bedroom to monitor his breathing. There was movement in and out of the house all night long. This night, my husband and I did not get any sleep. First, there was simply nowhere to sleep—all bedrooms were filled, all fold-out couches were filled, all bathtubs were occupied, and most of the floor space was gone too. So much was happening, but we had to at least monitor what was going on in our own home even if it was out of our control. As the stream of people came and went, but mostly kept coming, Sully and I were running from room to room, finding places for people to sleep, handing out pillows and sandwiches, and Jawana was happily running her own pattern through the house checking in with old friends and making new ones. At one point she came skipping through the room I was in and called out happily, "Mamma, Santa Claus is here." I turned to greet Greek Orthodox Archbishop Iakovos, who did indeed have an impressive beard as well as the insignia of his office.

As we travel through life, I believe we move by faith and our trust in God. We grow and learn, and are enlightened by what we experience—and through this movement our experiences were many. One of the memories that stands out like a beacon occurred the morning of the big march. I had always known what respect really meant, respect for a person, an ideology, or a religion, but I saw it firsthand that morning. I witnessed Rabbi Abraham Heschel of the Jewish Theological Seminary of America, a world scholar, setting up his prayer station on the coffee table in our living room. Archbishop Iakovos was also setting his prayer station on the mantel in the same room. Each man recognized and respected the other's beliefs. Others in the house gave the same respect by just sitting quietly or bowing their heads. They had spent the night in the living room, Rabbi Heschel on the couch and Archbishop Iakavos in a large chair with a pillow—the best I could offer!

I knew these men were important when I was first introduced to them, but it was later, after the march, that I really had time to focus and learn who they really were. On these occasions, I had a warm feeling pass through my body. These two religious leaders, the two Nobel Peace Prize winners, president of the AFL-CIO Walter Reuther, and many others were in our house. What harm could come to Sully, me, or Jawana with such people in the house by the side of the road?

28
Marching Orders

Another hectic morning—what do I cook? How many servings of grits do I make? Who eats eggs and cooked which way? Then the answer to these questions suddenly came. Cook what you have and hope it works for everyone. So I cooked a big pot of grits, fried several two-pound packages of bacon and several other pounds of sausage, boiled some eggs and scrambled several dozen others, and baked dozens of prepared breakfast rolls. I had to break my lifelong practice, as there were simply too many people to serve for me to have time to make homemade biscuits. I put all the food on the table and hoped for the best. It disappeared in a matter of minutes. Who all ate that morning I cannot testify to, but they all found me to say thanks for a wonderful breakfast. Then on to the next chore, which was cleaning up after the big breakfast. Stuff was everywhere! Thanks again to Dora and other staff who helped get the house in order for the next round of events.

Everybody dressed and received last-minute reports, with the phone ringing and the doorbell about to come off the wall and reporters trying to get in the whole time. Thank God I did not pull door duty that day! Some of the people in the house began to move on to the church and get a feel of what was going on and to mingle with the people.

Coretta and Juanita came early in the morning to join their husbands on the big day. I was truly glad to see them because their presence meant four more hands to help, and help they did. I remember all of us in our master bedroom while Ralph and Martin put on their marching boots. The air was once again happy, everyone was joking and feeling upbeat. Ralph was given a box with a new pair of marching boots and Martin was given his box. Martin turned to Ralph and said, "Ralph, you have the wrong box, these boots are too large for me, they must be yours since you have big feet." Ralph replied to Martin, "With these boots being new, before this day is over you will wish you were in the shoebox!" and everyone fell out with laughter. All worries were put on the back burner for just a little while. Everybody was ready, pictures were taken, and all the staff had been given the "go" sign. Now on to the church. The ladies and I made a path through the house one last time. I knew Martin had to fly out that night, and I also knew I had to get back home to prepare for those who would be returning to the house that evening.

Everybody finally left the house for the church to attend the enormous mass meeting where everybody was given their marching orders. Three hundred people had been selected as those who would march the entire fifty-mile route, and they were separated from everyone else. There was no way for everyone to fit into the church. The rest of us gathered outside the church to witness for ourselves the mass of humanity that had gathered. I demanded to go this time and I insisted that I would march. Bullhorns had to be used to communicate what to do to the mass of people outside. Never before had I seen so many people. Counting the people was simply impossible, and the reporters had to guess. I have read various accounts of the number over the years, but no one really knows because throughout the day people continued to come.

All lined up, we finally started for the bridge and then began the

crossing. I smiled to myself as I passed white men whose faces had
been red and twisted from shouting ugly names just a few days earlier
but now were standing quietly, and lawmen who were now there to
protect us. What an irony. All in their uniforms, clean-faced, guns
at their sides ready to protect us! I wondered what they must be feeling and thinking. Sometimes people have mixed emotions. In their
hearts they know what is right—or do they? Some of them also believe they must follow the majority for their own safety. They are
bound by dictates of their own environment, just as we are in ours
but for different reasons. Their beliefs are taught from birth. When
children are fed from birth a steady diet of hate and indifference, that
nourishment becomes part of their very being. Their parents, the extended family, and even the church convey the same negative lessons
and attitudes. What else can they know? Each generation teaches the
same lessons. What else can they feel?

Let me stop here and talk about a segment of our society that I
have long wondered about: religious people. I ask myself, do we serve
the same God? Do we read and believe in the same Bible? It has often
been said that 11:00 on Sunday morning is the most segregated hour
in America. Is it that we worship a different God? Or is it political
ideology? I thought we were to love our neighbor as ourselves, but
since there is a white neighborhood and a black neighborhood, does
this rule not apply in this case? Maybe the word "neighbor" in their
dictionaries has a different meaning than in the dictionary I have.
In my dictionary, and in reading and studying the Bible, I thought
"neighbor" meant all of God's children—the ones he created. "Do
unto others as you would have them do unto you." I guess when they
read "others," it does not include black people. God the Father sent
his only son to save us from ourselves and to give man a second chance,
but here again I guess this does not include black people. The hate

some seemingly God-fearing people carry around with them is not confined to black people; it seems to travel to anyone who is different. The Bible also states that we are all made in God's image. So how can black people be excluded from this rule? I ask you, are we so different and is there such a need to feel superior to other people that control and power become the focus of one's being? I continue to ponder these questions.

I marched beside Jean Young (Andy's wife) and their children. I did not take Jawana because we felt she was too young and the distance was too far for her to walk. Sully and I, however, walked and walked and walked. Once we were well on the way, Martin sent word back asking me to go back to the house to be there to receive phone calls. Shortly thereafter, a van came by carrying Dr. Bunche and several other older men back to Selma, so I jumped in and went home. This gave me a chance to do some picking up around the house. Paper plates from breakfast were still everywhere. (With so many people eating at any one time, I never tried to use china.) Dora McDonald soon came in and really helped me. During this period in the house I did not know what activity to plan for or the numbers I could expect. Martin, Coretta, Ralph, and Juanita walked to the campsite for the first night. After praying and seeing that the marchers were settled and safe, they returned to the house by the side of the road.

It was so humorous seeing and hearing them come in from a long march and a long day. Martin declared the feet he was walking on could not belong to him. He laughed and continued to complain he could not bend over to remove his boots. Someone helped him take his boots off. Martin then stated, "Those were the hardest boots I have ever worn." Ralph reminded him, "I told you this morning you would wish your feet had been in the box those boots came in before the day was over!" I quickly put together yet another meal for the hungry and tired crew. Some staff began to filter in, bringing encouraging reports from the march site. Dr. King and Reverend Abernathy were pleased to hear that things had gone so well throughout the day. Ralph said, "I wonder what George Wallace is thinking now, with us marching on his highway with his National Guard watching over us."

Can you imagine Dr. King receiving dignitaries at the kitchen table with his feet in a tub of hot water? Ralph then came into the kitchen and asked, "Where is my foot tub? My feet hurt, too." I thought for a moment and realized I did not have another small tub. Suddenly, a solution came to me; I pulled the turkey roaster out of the cabinet, put some hot water in it, and made a second foot tub! This brought another round of laughter. Martin told Ralph, "Your feet are so big, Jean had to bring out her biggest pan to fit your feet." Laughter broke out again as the joke traveled throughout the house. Ralph took his foot tub and quietly left the room to find another room to soak in. The mood of the group was elevated because of a very successful day. Those who could not march all the way came by to congratulate Martin and Ralph on the day and a job well done, and also expressed their appreciation for being able to come to Selma to be a part of this historic day.

Knowing Martin had to leave for a speaking engagement, some of the staff came in for another staff meeting. I thought the house by the side of the road had been busy, but after the march, activity was at an even higher pitch. Plans continued to be firmed up for the rest of the march into Montgomery, to deal with any trouble that had come about, and to try to anticipate any problems that might arise.

29
A Concert for the Masses

During this last meeting the day of the march, Martin asked me to go to Montgomery to help Dora McDonald pull together a gala celebration that would be held for the arriving marchers at St. Jude Catholic School in Montgomery. St. Jude is a large complex on Highway 80 at the entrance to Montgomery coming from Selma. The complex contains a hospital, church, school, doctors' offices, and administrative buildings. In addition, the grounds are large enough to stage a large gathering.

Martin had asked Harry Belafonte, a longtime supporter and consummate entertainer, to arrange this event. Belafonte was not seeking any headlines or publicity, he just wanted to do whatever he could for the movement, and most of all he did it for his dear friend Martin Luther King Jr. Belafonte had called the house many times to talk with Martin, Ralph, or Andy, and if I answered the phone I would immediately recognize his velvet voice. What a pleasure it would be to finally see the man behind that voice!

When Dora McDonald and I got to Montgomery on the Wednesday after the march began, we went to the historic Greystone Hotel where rooms had been reserved for us. We had traveled along State Highway 14 from Selma, what we called the "back way" to Montgomery, which meant we did not see the marchers on their journey down Highway 80. Once at the hotel, we were greeted by none other than Harry Belafonte, who was (besides Sully of course) the most gracious, kind, gallant, handsome, wonderful man I had ever met. He was all of these things and then some! Dora introduced us and I told him I was the one who had received his calls for Dr. King in Selma. Now get ready for this picture: Mr. Belafonte bowed at the waist, kissed my hand, and thanked me for coming to Montgomery to help. He kissed my hand. I promised myself I would not wash that spot for days!

We were there to check the arrival and departure times of the entertainers and to make sure they were picked up at the airport and brought to the hotel, and to alert Mr. Belafonte when they had arrived. We also had to transport the performers to St. Jude near the time they would appear onstage and then take them back to the airport to catch their flight out.

Sully and I had planned for him to join me in Montgomery on Thursday to be with me to meet and greet the stars before the big show. He came as planned but with me moving around the hotel so much, he decided to sit in the hotel lobby and watch the stars as they came in. While sitting there, he noticed some men in cowboy hats stringing wires in and around the lobby. He decided they were local television station technicians who had come to the hotel to film the stars as they came into the hotel.

Still sitting and saying to himself, "There is Nipsy Russell, here comes Peter, Paul, and Mary," and so on, his attention was diverted from star-watching to seeing some Montgomery police come into the hotel. Now Sully was wondering, what in the world is going on and where is my wife? Something here does not smell right. After finding me we returned to the lobby in time to see the police handcuffing and arresting the men he thought were part of television crews. The police rounded up all of the wires that had been placed with tape on the floors all over the hotel. Then we were told the men had come to wire the hotel to bomb the entire structure!

The plan was to be carried out in broad daylight. Here again, another brush with death. Sully remarked on how polite the men had been while they were taping wire around the chair he was sitting in!

The police carried the men in their big cowboy hats off just as quietly and as quickly as they had come in. Many of the stars and others never knew the danger that was averted that day. One of the policemen told my husband, "If we had just been ten minutes later in arriving, everyone would have gone up in smoke!"

My husband said to me, "Let's go home now. It's bad enough to be threatened at home, but to get bumped off in the lobby of the Greystone would be a bit much." But we still had a job to do. The show must go on at the appointed time. We began to load some of the scheduled entertainers onto the bus for the ride to St. Jude, where an outdoor stage had been erected. There we saw Burt Lancaster, Shelley Winters, Tony Bennett, Joan Baez, Dick Gregory, Pernell Roberts, Sammy Davis Jr., James Baldwin, Peter Lawford, Leonard Bernstein, and many others.

After a third roundtrip to St. Jude, I told my husband that I was tired and wanted to return to Selma. I had been as close to the stars as I cared to be. Even the marchers wouldn't be able to get this close and personal. Let's go home. He agreed and we arrived back at the now quiet hotel as all of the activity had shifted to St. Jude. I gathered my bag and we began to figure out a way to get out of town. We decided to go the most traveled route on Highway 80 because going back the less traveled way might not be too safe this particular night. We quietly passed the site of the gala, wished them well, and headed back to the house by the side of the road. How glad we were to be home!

We did not realize how close we had come to danger once again as we traveled home on Highway 80. Many people had gone to the concluding concert and now needed to get back to Selma, especially the three hundred or so marchers who had walked the entire fifty miles.

Many people had signed up to drive their cars to and from Montgomery to ferry people back to Selma. One of those volunteers was a white mother of five children from Detroit named Viola Liuzzo. She had come down to help make this a better world for her children, for our daughter, Jawana, and for all the children in the world. She believed in the goals of the movement and did what she could to help. After bringing one carload to Selma, she was returning to Montgomery for another load of passengers. She never made it. A car with nightriders pulled up beside her car and began shooting to kill and this night they were successful. All because she was a white woman with a heart that was in the right place. I believe God gives some of us special missions when we are born. Then there are people like Viola Liuzzo who are sent here by God to reveal to us man's inhumanity to man. She may have been a link to bigger and better things to come. I like to think so.

We had been in the house about twenty minutes before the awful shot was fired. A call came into the house to inform us that there was real danger tonight and that Mrs. Luizzo had been killed. We were totally alone in the house. This would be the perfect opportunity for evildoers to hit us in anger for all we had done for the movement. We could just hear the sentiment. We had made a safe home for that "nigger and communist" Martin Luther King (those yelling that Martin was a communist didn't even understand what the term meant let alone the ideology behind the concept). Sully and I felt we needed to batten down the hatches and at least be careful. But here I am, many years later, able to tell this story, thanks be to God.

In honor of the movement there have been thousands of streets renamed, statues crafted, and buildings named, but one such memorial came from the efforts of Mrs. Evelyn Lowery, Dr. Joseph Lowery's wife, on Highway 80 where Viola Liuzzo was killed. The SCLC Women decided several years ago to memorialize the spot where Mrs. Luizzo met her tragic death. A marble piece stands in her honor like a beacon up on a knoll overlooking where she died and shines in the sunlight to honor the life she gave. SCLC Women will not forget her. They continue to improve the site as time goes on so that future generations will know. Once you have made it into the hearts of people, you will never be forgotten. As long as there are history books to be read and people remember what was accomplished at Selma, Viola Liuzzo will never be forgotten.

30
The Final Journey

After the national attention on the Selma movement moved on to other struggles and other places, our life changed completely. We knew something very important had happened, and we would somehow never be the same, but it would take years for us to begin to realize what had happened that spring. At first we were just relieved that the telephone had stopped ringing constantly, that we could move about our house without fear of falling over some exhausted staff member asleep under the kitchen table or running into a delegation of local leaders streaming in the back door. I had to stop and think when cooking for just my family, what portions should I use?

We could sleep in our own beds again and look out the front windows without the view being blocked by reporters on the porch. We also began to understand a bit of what had happened, now that we could stop and think. Had it all been in vain, would matters just slide back to the way they had been, now that the leaders and the cameras and all the attention had moved on? The local segregationists, the local white powers were all still there. They hadn't left with the media and the movement leaders. Yes, the president had promised voting rights laws on TV and with the whole country watching. But he was in Washington, the TV people were in New York, and we were in

Selma. Had anything really changed? When Jawana was old enough, would she vote, serve on a jury, be addressed politely in the courthouse?

The three of us were just settling back into our old routines, and getting used to quiet in the house that spring afternoon when Martin showed up unannounced at the back door.

"Martin, come in, we'll see no one bothers you here."

He went into the middle bedroom, got his usual pajamas, took a shower, and began to relax. The question burning on my lips was "Does anyone know where you are?" The answer came slowly. "No." My next question was going to be, "Do I need to call someone?" But my mind cautioned me to let it alone for now. I told him to go to bed and that he did. I took out the phone in his room and moved the other phones within hearing distance away, and closed off that part of the house so it could be as quiet as possible.

After I was sure he was in bed I turned back to the kitchen and a fright came over me that I could hardly imagine. He had driven all the way here alone. The more I thought about it the more frightened I became. If he had been recognized on the highway or in the city limits of Selma, what could have happened! His old blue Pontiac was parked in the backyard but at least it was out of sight of the street. His car looked like thousands of others, so maybe no one would notice, especially since this car was not seen during the time of the movement in Selma.

I went to the phone to call my husband at his office, and whispered, "Can you come home now?"

"Why, what's wrong?" he asked.

"Nothing, we are all right, just come home please."

He arrived within a few minutes. Coming into the driveway he saw Martin's car and asked, "What's going on?" Keeping my voice low, I told him what happened. We decided to leave Martin alone and maybe we would get some answers later; he had said he wanted to rest and so we let him sleep. I peeped into his room and he was out like a light. This all happened about 3:00 in the afternoon.

We woke up at 2:00 A.M., which in any other home would be considered the middle of the night, but not in this house. I have always teased my husband by telling him that he exists during the day but really comes alive at night! I guess Sully's habit of being a night owl began because of his playing in different night clubs to put himself through dental school and having worked the eleven-to-seven shift at the Delco Remy automobile plant in Indiana when he was just out of high school. So there is always activity late at night in the house by the side of the road. My husband goes to bed right after dinner every night and awakens around 10:00 P.M. for another four- to five-hour stretch!

So when Martin woke up that night we were already up as usual, and I began cooking, knowing what we had had for dinner was not going to be appropriate at two in the morning. So I began to cook grits, eggs, bacon, and hot biscuits, and made coffee. I have already told you I make biscuits from scratch, just as I also do with cakes and pies. I tried to be the best homemaker I could be. When we were first married, as a young wife I tried to impress my husband by cooking meals from scratch. After that, I never could get away with serving food out of a can. Sully would always say when I did try to serve him canned biscuits, "You did not make these, did you."

Eating and talking, Martin told us just how tired he was, the many pressures on him, and the accusations and personal attacks even from friends and supporters. He felt that at the house by the side of the road he could get the quiet understanding and simple friendship he needed. I did not know who knew he was here; after all, he was a grown man. We talked and ate until I noticed the sun was coming up. After a while he seemed to really relax. Finally we all went to bed, although my rest was to be short-lived because our daughter, who had been asleep all night, would soon be up. I decided when she awoke to take her to Ban Dam's house for the day. Later when Martin woke up again I cooked him yet another meal.

That day my husband decided to stay home. He called his office and canceled all his appointments because he felt he needed to be at home for Martin. During our long conversations into the afternoon and evening that day, Martin asked us to consider moving to Atlanta, where the rest of the crowd—Ralph and Juanita, Creecy and Margaurite, Jean and Andy, plus Coretta and himself—lived. Out of the members of the three churches they pastored, and other ministers he knew, he assured Sully that he could have a good dental practice in Atlanta. He talked for some time about his plan, trying to persuade my husband to no avail. I was willing to move, but the breadwinner thought not. His rationale was there were only two black dentists in the Selma area (the other was also a relative of mine), we both had close family in Selma, and our roots ran very deep in this soil and the community.

We did not see Martin very much after that visit. He moved onto other vineyards to do what he could to right the problems of our country. We saw him a few times in Atlanta in the years that followed. After a while people would come by the house and ask if they could just come in and look around. They would always promise not to touch anything. During the late 1970s reporters began to come and ask questions about what went on in the house by the side of the road. Historians also came until all of this traffic became a problem. I finally had to put an end to this activity because when I would see the finished product, it was nothing like what I had said. They printed someone else's views or slants on what I said, or they wanted me to say what I would not say or did not know.

Even though we did not see much of Martin, we continued to see Ralph, who would always come through Selma on his way to visit his family in his hometown. I remember some time after the Selma movement, Ralph's family had a large reunion and we were invited to attend and did. Whenever Ralph was anywhere in the neighborhood, he came by to see us and have dinner, for which I always tried to have steamed cabbage and parsley potatoes, two of his favorites! He also liked black-eyed peas, okra, and cornbread. Ralph was always on a diet that Juanita had put him on. But when he came here he left the diet at the back door. He always asked me, with a big smile on his face, "When you talk to Juanita please do not tell her what I ate or how much!"

We read and watched as Martin and Ralph moved all over the country, advocating for social issues that would eventually change the world, city by city, issue by issue. I was always afraid that something would happen. It seems to me now as if after the Selma movement was over, I became fearful of what could have happened to us and what must lie ahead for Martin and Ralph.

On the evening of April 4, 1968, after eating dinner, Sully, Jawana, and I were relaxing while watching television in the living room when the phone rang. My husband answered and heard the voice of his best friend, Johnny Brown, on the other end saying, "Have you heard? Martin Luther King has been shot in Memphis." Sully yelled, "No! Man, what are you talking about?" Hanging up the phone, he repeated the conversation to us and at about the same instant all of the television stations began to break into their programs with the announcement. Walter Cronkite gave the chilling report: "Dr. Martin Luther King Jr. has been shot in Memphis, Tennessee."

We sat frozen in disbelief. Then the questions began: who, what, where, how bad was it, and all the rest. Finally, I said, "I want this confirmed." By this time the phone really began to ring with call after call. We finally had to accept the reality that Martin was gone.

All of the memories came flooding through my mind, too many for me to sort through in one evening. We began to remember the feeling that Martin had that he would be killed. We had talked about this possibility during some of our quiet times together. He was sure that it would happen sometime, and he hoped he would be ready and that his name was written in the Lamb's Book of Life and that God would receive him.

What do we do now? My wonderful, thoughtful husband said, "We will mourn him in our hearts and thank God that he let Martin come by here. We must talk about him to our eight-year-old daughter to help her understand what has happened to Uncle Martin and why." This we knew would be a hard job; we did not have any of the answers but we would have to tell her about it anyway.

Oftentimes children understand or can cut to the essentials much better than adults. "Mamma, Uncle Martin has gone to live with God, he can rest, and he does not have to worry about marching anymore." Somehow we made it through that black night. The next day, fearing she still did not understand because I could not, I asked Jawana to write down her feelings about Uncle Martin's death. She went to her room, got some construction paper, and began to write: "Uncle Martin was a good man and we loved him. He was a good friend of my Mamma and Daddy. He called me his niece and I called him Uncle Martin. He tried to help a lot of people and now he has gone to live with God." I realized she understood when I saw that her writing was in the past tense. I still have her piece of paper somewhere in the house by the side of the road.

Randolph Blackwell, an SCLC staff member, phoned saying he was calling for Coretta, asking if we could join her for a private family viewing in Atlanta. What could we say? We would be there. We arrived at Sister's Chapel on Spelman University's campus and joined the family as they were going in. The body was already in place; we stood back to allow the immediate family, Coretta, Martin's sister Christine, and others, to go in first. Following Coretta and Christine were Daddy and Mamma King, and then Sully and I were signaled to go ahead. It was very difficult for us to see Daddy King overcome with such grief, wanting to hold his son once again. He lunged to pick Martin's body up out of the casket, not realizing the casket had an inner seal with a glass cover. My husband and another friend, Robert Williams, who was at the time head of the music department at Grambling College in Louisiana, were standing near Daddy King as he moved toward the casket, almost knocking it to the floor and losing his balance.

After viewing the body, we embraced the others who were gathered and expressed how we felt. Friendship, love, respect, grief.

Later my husband and I sat in the chapel together trying to deal with our own grief and to comfort each other. We finally said goodbye to our dear friend Martin Luther King Jr. and left to return to Selma that night down a long, dark highway.

Riding back there was quite a conversation between us: "Do you remember when." On and on the memories flowed, then we were quiet, sadness in our hearts, facing the truth that we were saying our final good-byes. Back in Selma and dealing with our own sadness, we knew Martin's funeral would be so large and attended by so many dignitaries that we would be swallowed up in the crowd, so we wouldn't try to go. That's the way we would leave it.

On Saturday, to our surprise, we received a telegram, which was our invitation to attend the funeral on April 9. I remember calling Juanita Abernathy to ask her what the telegram meant. She told me there would be two funerals, one for the family and close friends and one for the public. If we received a telegram that meant we were to attend the private family funeral. Now we would have to return to Atlanta.

Upon arrival we went to Martin and Coretta's house on Sunset Avenue. We needed to check in and get instructions regarding where to be and when. After mingling with friends and family, I was told I could go into Coretta's bedroom and speak privately with her. In their bedroom while she was still dressing for the funeral, Juanita and I offered whatever support we could. Suddenly the door opened and Jacqueline Kennedy came in to embrace Coretta. Mrs. Kennedy brought grace, dignity, and calm into the room with the resolve of another great lady who knew all too well the feelings Coretta was experiencing.

We spoke, shook hands, and introduced ourselves to Mrs. Kennedy. Feeling the kinship between the two women whose husbands had been taken away by an assassin's bullet, I felt I should leave the room so whatever needed to be said between these two ladies could be said in private. I held the hand of Coretta Scott King and Jacqueline Kennedy and then quietly left the room.

Sully and I soon left the house for Ebenezer Baptist Church, holding the telegram in my hand because we had been told only invited persons would be allowed into the church. After getting through the throngs of people outside we were finally seated. As I looked around, to my right sat the Kennedy family, behind me sat Sidney Poitier, Sammy Davis Jr., Diana Ross, and Eartha Kitt. The church seemed to be filled with remarkable people from all walks of life. Many of the entertainers were those who had come to St. Jude's in

Montgomery in 1965 in answer to Martin's call to celebrate the march from Selma. Not far from us sat the U.S. government delegation, with Vice President Hubert H. Humphrey representing President Johnson. There were also several senators and representatives in this section. Then my husband turned to me and quietly said, "With all of these dignitaries, how did we make it in?" I answered, "True friends stand in a category all their own." Then my eyes fell on Mahalia Jackson. What words would she sing on this day of sorrow to remember her dear friend Martin Luther King Jr.? May God be with all of us this day! Sully and I were about six benches behind the immediate family. I could see Bernice as she sat on her mother's lap, and the other children, Yolanda, Martin III, and Dexter, at her side.

I wondered what fear and sorrow must have been going through their young minds. They had spent such precious little time with their father on a day-to-day basis, and now he was gone and they would never see him again. They would never have his gentle and loving hand touch them as they grew up—all because of hate. After the service we made plans to watch the funeral procession while sitting on the Creecy's front porch. The procession would pass right in front of the Creecy's church and their home, which was located next door to the church. There we all watched this part of the funeral together with our children, saying good-bye again to our dear friend.

My heart really went out to Ralph that day. His dear and close friend was gone. I knew what a toll the funeral would take on him. He somehow had to pick up the mantle from Martin and carry on, doing the work that he and Martin had done together for so long, from the beginning and the Montgomery Bus Boycott. He would have to take over the presidency of SCLC. Which path must he take? There were threats on his life, too. All of this must have been going through his mind as he prepared to bury Martin. Would the organizations and people rally around him as they did Martin? I often felt Ralph did not really have time to mourn. The garbage workers strike in Memphis that had brought Martin there was still going on. There were also plans for the Poor People's March to be held in Washington, D.C. Plan after plan to ponder, organize, lead. Ralph also had to think about the safety and well-being of his own family and his moral obligation to look after Martin's family. Can you imagine the weight on this man's shoulders?

Dr. Billy Kyle, a prominent Memphis minister, made a profound statement after Martin's death: "He gave his life for the garbage workers." Does this statement remind you of another statement made thousands of years ago: "What you do for the least of my children, this you have done unto me."

James Earl Ray is the name given to the man suspected of killing Martin Luther King Jr. There are, however, many questions about whether he did this terrible deed alone or as the tool of unknown others, just as there are questions as to whether Lee Harvey Oswald shot President Kennedy. Ray later tried to recant his statement that he shot Martin Luther King Jr., but by then nobody would listen.

Ray died in 1998, and his story was never told in a court of law. I never believed he killed Martin, at least not alone. For me there are too many unanswered questions about the case. Where did Ray, a small-time loser and petty thief, get the high-powered tools and means to travel around the country? Why did the FBI not look into any of the other leads? We may never know the real story.

31
Memories and Echoes of Martin

After the funeral procession, we spent the night at the Creecy's home and the next day returned to Selma and the house filled with so many memories of our dear friend. We have consciously or unconsciously saved items, chosen not to have furniture recovered, all in an unspoken attempt to retain the presence of our friend Martin. Finally, years later, I could not stand the carpet in one of the bedrooms any longer; it was worn out and unraveling! I had the carpet replaced where staff had sat, Martin had talked and spilled cough medicine, and many had slept.

I can walk through any room of this house and in my mind's eye remember and see activity. I will see something on television that will trigger a memory or something in the newspaper or a magazine that will make me recall an event in the house.

Maybe we need another movement, over forty years later, this time focusing on the needs of the people, such as education reform, health, the economy, the global environment, and rebuilding America. Let me stop here and explain what I mean by a movement today. If the government will not provide for its citizens, the legal system does not treat all persons fairly, and the church is still segregated, not welcoming certain people into their flocks, then the people have to find a way to be heard. If no one is listening, the people have to make themselves heard. Young people have limited access to a college education, and many of our youth do not finish high school. Jobs are going overseas and the standard of living for Americans is rapidly deteriorating. With no jobs comes no hope. What will we leave for the next generations? Maybe we need another movement that will benefit all the citizens of this great country and not just a privileged few. A movement that will make education, economic success, and religious freedom equally attainable and accessible to all.

In this country power and money make the mare trot. Power is money and money is power. The past movements made us look at ourselves and seek a better world for all to exist. We have made many changes and we still have a long way to march.

Common issues of today are being discussed by individuals and groups, all with different agendas and styles in an attempt to bring the message of justice and freedom to America. People of color in this country and around the globe have endured generations of hardships. But now we must join the world and make our communities better for the future existence of everyone. All of the dreams of America have not been met, and the founding fathers knew the riches America holds and hoped that we would establish justice and freedom here first and then be a shining example for the world to see. This was Martin's dream, too. God will somehow send a leader for the people, and he or she will pull the voices together and make a difference. I believe Martin Luther King Jr. was such a leader sent to help his people and all of humanity.

Most of the men who were central figures in the civil rights movement are now gone to receive their just reward from their maker. My beloved husband, Sully, died in 2004. Seldom does a day go by that I am not filled with memories of my love for him and the times when we watched as history was indeed made in this country and in our house. Sully and I loved each other unconditionally, raised a wonderful daughter, and were privileged to play a small part in making this world a better place. What more can a young girl from Mobile, Alabama, ask?

We have also lost many of the women who stood behind the men. Coretta's death in 2006 made us all pause. After Martin's death, she spent the next forty years championing Martin's causes and making sure we would never forget his legacy. The rest of us are watching our children and grandchildren make their way in this world filled with all its joys and pains.

We cannot all be a Martin Luther King Jr., but each and every one of us can make a positive difference in the lives of our families and the people we meet each day. For you see the dream is still alive.

Selma, Alabama, the city that gave us the voting rights movement, has not done as well as it should have. Before the movement, Selma was the Dallas County seat and the hub of the area. While in recent years we have had a black mayor, the town in some respects is still very much divided along racial lines. Many whites, including almost all of the Jewish population, have left the town. The whites that remain now choose to educate their children in all-white private schools— leaving the city schools for black children. The one high school in Selma is currently nearly completely black. The few white students who attend Selma High School are those whose parents cannot afford to send their children elsewhere. The economy is poor due to a loss of jobs and industry in the area that began in the early 1970s. City government and services are suffering from budget and management problems too numerous to discuss. Selma is a fractured city trying to deal with its past while struggling for the future. We still have not learned to "love thy neighbor as thyself." What we are taught at birth remains with us throughout our lives. If we are taught to love then love is what we will do. If we are taught to hate then hate is what we will do.

In walking around this house I often wonder if I could go through this experience again. Do the walls of this house have room enough to absorb more activity? This house still stands tall as a constant beacon for friends and all who come through its doors. What will the next movement be? What problems will need to be solved by the people for future generations? Life will go on. My only hope is that God will allow me to continue to work in his vineyard from the house by the side of the road!

Appendix One

Selma and Area Counties

Selma
Alabama

Key
1. Selma University
2. Brown's AME Chapel Church
3. Dallas County Courthouse
4. Edmund Pettus Bridge
5. House by the side of the road

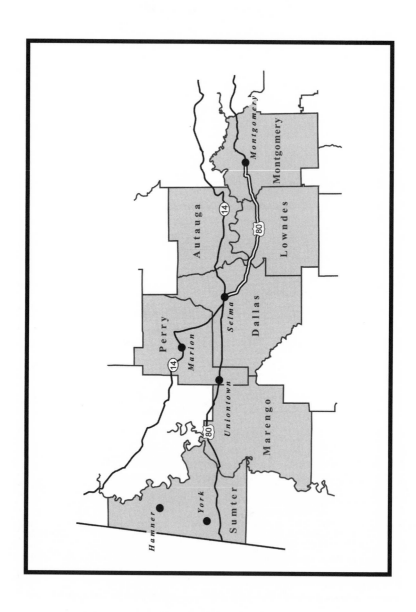

Appendix Two

Timeline for the Selma Voting Rights Campaign of 1965

1958 September: After receiving a summons, Dr. Sullivan Jackson and five other black Selma citizens testified before the U.S. Civil Rights Commission in Montgomery on barriers to voting in Selma.

1962 November: John Doar of the U.S. Justice Department visits Selma as part of a tour researching southern voting conditions.

1964 July: Selma Judge James A. Hare issues an injunction against demonstrations.

1964 October 5: Joseph (J. T.) Smitherman is sworn in as mayor of Selma. He creates the office of director of public safety to supervise police and fire departments in the city, a position then filled by Wilson Baker.

1964 October 15: Dr. Martin Luther King visits Selma and speaks at a Voters League meeting. King and the Southern Christian Leadership Conference (SCLC, founded by King in 1957) begin plans for a voting rights campaign in Selma, where less than 2 percent of eligible black citizens are registered (approximately 335 African-Americans registered out of an estimated 32,700 black eligible voters).

1964 November 11: During a retreat in Birmingham, Selma activists appeal to the SCLC to convince King to come to Selma to support the voting rights campaign. Ralph Abernathy supports the idea.

1964 December: King is awarded the Nobel Peace Prize, the youngest person ever to receive one.

1965 January 2: King and Abernathy visit Selma to assess the situation and launch the voting rights campaign with a rally at Brown Chapel.

1965 January 5: President Lyndon Johnson lists voting rights for all citizens as a priority during his State of the Union address.

1965 January 18 (morning): Selma restaurants voluntarily integrate, in response to the Supreme Court ruling that the Civil Rights Act is constitutional.

King returns to Selma with aides and supporters. After attempting to join applicants at the county registrar they are turned away but not arrested.

At a rally King threatens to fill the jails unless blacks are permitted to register to vote. Plans are made to move the campaign to Camden, where *no* blacks are registered, if the next day's march in Selma is not successful. King later learns that Dallas sheriff Jim Clark has threatened to arrest "every goddamn one" of the protestors. King registers as a guest in Selma's Hotel Albert, the first black to do so, and is assaulted in the lobby by a white supremacist from Birmingham.

1965 January 19: King sends volunteers to attempt to register, protest, and accept imprisonment; 64 are arrested for "unlawful assembly" at the courthouse.

1965 January 22: 100 black schoolteachers, led by F. D. Reese, rally at the Dallas County Courthouse for the right to vote.

Civil rights attorneys request an injunction to restrain Sheriff Clark and county officials from harassing applicants attempting to register to vote.

1965 January 23: Judge Daniel Thomas grants an injunction to restrain Clark.

1965 January 25: During a demonstration at the courthouse, Sheriff

Clark grabs Annie Cooper, a black woman, and in the ensuing melee Clark needs the help of three deputies and his billy club to subdue her. Cooper spends eleven hours in jail. Photographs of a bleeding Annie Cooper are publicized nationally.

1965 February 1: King and at least 260 others, many of them protesting schoolchildren, are arrested and jailed for "parading without a permit."

1965 February 2: 505 arrested.

1965 February 3: 331 arrested. Of the 1,286 arrests to date, 1,175 have been of teenagers.

1965 February 4: Judge Thomas enjoins registrars to cease discriminatory tactics in response to voter registration efforts.

1965 February 5: King writes from the Selma jail, "There are more Negroes in jail with me than there are on the voting rolls," a letter reproduced in the *New York Times*. By this time about 2,400 have been arrested. After conferring with U.S. attorney Nicholas Katzenbach (who would be named Attorney General on February 11), King posts bond and is released.

Malcolm X, also in Selma for a visit, speaks at Brown Chapel, along with Fred Shuttlesworth of Birmingham and Coretta Scott King.

1965 February 9: King meets with President Johnson in Washington, urging progress on voting rights legislation.

1965 February 10: Sheriff Clark forces 165 arrested black teenagers to walk to the armory where they will be incarcerated, followed by patrol cars. Pressure from the sheriff's cars and posse, armed with cattle prods, forces many of the youths to run much of the way. This enrages the black community; even the local Selma newspaper denounces the action.

1965 February 16: Sheriff Clark confronts C. T. Vivian on a march to the courthouse; Vivian lectures the deputies, who stop to listen. Enraged, Clark steps forward and strikes Vivian, breaking a bone in his own hand.

1965 February 18: Sensing momentum and eventual victory in the campaign, SCLC decides to shift effort in Selma to the hiring of black police and sheriff's deputies and to move the voting rights campaigns to nearby rural Perry, Wilcox, and Lowndes counties.

James Orange is arrested in Marion (Perry County seat) for a voting rights demonstration.

Five hundred blacks attempt the first march at night, to the courthouse, which ends in an attack on the marchers by local and state police. Eight are later hospitalized (five blacks and three white reporters).

Local marcher Jimmie Lee Jackson is shot by a state trooper and is refused treatment by the local hospital where he had been working earlier that day.

826 blacks are charged with unlawful assembly, and Gov. George Wallace blames "communist agitators" for the unrest.

1965 February 26: Jimmie Lee Jackson dies in Selma.

1965 March 1: King leads a march of 350 to the courthouse.

1965 March 2: 700 attend the memorial service for Jimmie Lee Jackson in Marion.

1965 March 3: King speaks to 2,000 at the Jimmie Lee Jackson memorial service in Selma and announces the plan to march on Montgomery.

1965 March 6: Wallace prohibits a march on Montgomery and orders state police to prevent it.

Joseph Ellwanger, a white Lutheran minister from Birmingham, leads 60 other whites on a march to the Dallas County courthouse to support voting rights. Police restrain a white mob of 500 from attacking them.

1965 March 7, "Bloody Sunday" (morning): After consulting with Abernathy and King, who are in Atlanta, Hosea Williams decides to hold a march that morning, rather than the original plan to conduct the march on the following Tuesday.

(Afternoon): Hosea Williams and John Lewis lead protesters from Brown Chapel to the bridge, intending to kneel and pray and return to the church but are attacked by about 90 state troopers and the Dallas County sheriff's posse after crossing the Edmund Pettus Bridge. Fifty-six blacks, including Lewis, are hospitalized with injuries.

National TV carries film of the attack during prime time.

In response, King, who had been in Atlanta that morning, calls on religious leaders to join him in Selma.

1965 March 8: King, Abernathy, and John Doar from the U.S. Department of Justice visit injured John Lewis in hospital.

Boston Unitarian minister James Reeb is among clergymen who respond to King's call.

SNCC and SCLC leaders meet at the Jackson home to decide the next move; King announces at an evening Brown Chapel rally that the march would begin again on Tuesday, March 9.

1965 March 9: Doar meets with King at the Jackson residence to attempt to delay a new march until an injunction to prevent attacks by police can be secured.

450 clergymen and 2,000 African Americans march to the Pettus bridge and pray at the site of the March 7 attack, and then return to Brown Chapel. Many marchers had assumed they would again attempt to reach Montgomery, but leaders decide they need more time to organize and secure court authority to march.

Reeb and others are attacked by whites that evening. Reeb is mortally injured.

1965 March 10: Rev. L. L. Anderson leads 500 marchers from Brown Chapel to a roadblock set up by Selma mayor Joe Smitherman and Public Safety director Wilson Baker. Marchers spend two hours in prayer at the barrier.

1965 March 11: Reeb dies of his injuries.

Judge Johnson is petitioned to authorize the march on Montgomery and orders the State of Alabama to protect it.

1965 March 13: Ignoring a personal appeal from George Wallace, President Johnson announces he will propose voting rights legislation.

1965 March 15: King speaks at Reeb's memorial service in Brown Chapel; 2,000 march to the courthouse. That evening President Johnson makes a televised address to a joint session of Congress in support of the voting rights bill. King, Lewis, Vivian, and other movement staff watch the broadcast from the Jackson home living room.

1965 March 16: King and Lewis march in Montgomery with SNCC leaders to protest police violence in that city.

1965 March 17: Judge Frank Johnson grants permission for the march from Selma to Montgomery.

1965 March 19: The cover of *Life* shows armed Alabama troopers awaiting marchers in Selma.

1965 March 21: 3,200 protesters begin the march down Highway 80 toward Montgomery. Under the protection of 1,800 federalized National Guardsmen, 2,000 U.S. Army troops, 100 FBI agents, and 100 U.S. marshals, 250 selected marchers went the whole way. March leaders place people from Selma at the head of the procession. Also at the front are Coretta and Martin Luther King, A. Philip Randolph, Ralph Bunche, Ralph and Juanita Abernathy, Andy and Jean Young, Jim Foreman, Hosea Williams, Dick Gregory, John Lewis, Rabbi Abraham Heschel, John Doar, Ramsey Clark, and Jimmie Lee Jackson's grandfather Cager Lee.

1965 March 25: Marchers arrive in Montgomery; 25,000 demonstrators join the Selma marchers for a rally at the state capitol, addressed by King. The rally ends at a huge outdoor concert, organized by Harry Belafonte.

Later that night Viola Liuzzo, a Detroit housewife, is shot dead as she helps drive marchers home to Selma from Montgomery.

1965 March 26: *Life* cover shows King holding a wreath for James

Reeb accompanied by UAW president Walter Reuther and Greek Orthodox archbishop Iakovos and others.

1965 August 6: Lyndon Johnson signs the 1965 Voting Rights Act into law.

1965 September 2: Sheriff Clark is found guilty of violating a restraining order for the February 10 forced march and is fined $1,500.

1966 November: Aided by black votes, Wilson Baker defeats Jim Clark for sheriff.

1967 November: In the fall elections an estimated 10,000 black voters are registered in Dallas County, about 50 percent of the electorate.

Many good books exist on the civil rights movement, but the following were particularly helpful in constructing the timeline.

Branch, Taylor. *At Canaan's Edge: America in the King Years, 1965–68.* Simon and Schuster, 2006.

Gaillard, Frye. *Cradle of Freedom: Alabama and the Movement That Changed America.* University of Alabama Press, 2004.

Lewis, John, with Michael D'Orso. *Walking with the Wind: A Memoir of the Movement.* Harcourt Brace, 1998.

McWhorter, Diane. *Carry Me Home: Birmingham, Alabama, the Climactic Battle of the Civil Rights Revolution.* Simon and Schuster, 2001.

Thornton, J. Mills. *Dividing Lines: Municipal Politics and the Struggle for Civil Rights in Montgomery, Birmingham, and Selma.* University of Alabama Press, 2002.

Appendix Three

CABBAGE RECIPE
3 tablespoons bacon drippings
1 medium cabbage
¾ cup bell pepper, chopped coarsely
¾ cup celery, chopped coarsely
1 cup yellow onion, chopped coarsely
1 teaspoon salt
1 teaspoon black pepper

Heat bacon drippings or fry 3 or 4 strips of bacon to get drippings. Add remaining ingredients to heated skillet, adding ¾ cup of water. Put lid on skillet to steam over medium to low heat. Stirring occasionally, cook about 10 minutes. Cooking time may differ according to type of stove; may take less time. Do not overcook.